The Cast Iron *Chef*

Main Courses

By Matt Pelton

CFI
Springville, Utah

This is not an official publication of The Church of Jesus Christ of Latter-day Saints. The opinions and views expressed herein belong solely to the author and do not necessarily represent the opinions or views of Cedar Fort, Inc. Permission for the use of sources, graphics, and photos is also solely the responsibility of the author.

ISBN 13: 978-1-59955-135-7

Published by CFI, an imprint of Cedar Fort, Inc., 2373 W. 700 S., Springville, UT, 84663
Distributed by Cedar Fort, Inc. www.cedarfort.com

LIBRARY OF CONGRESS CATALOGING-IN-PUBLICATION DATA

Pelton, Matt (Matthew)
  The cast iron chef / Matt Pelton.
    p. cm.
  ISBN 978-1-59955-135-7
  1. Dutch oven cookery. I. Title.
  TX840.D88P45 2008
  641.5'89—dc22
                        2007052894

Cover design by Jeremy Beal
Cover design © 2008 by Lyle Mortimer
Edited and typeset by Lyndsee Simpson Cordes

Printed in the United States of America

10 9 8 7 6 5 4 3 2 1

Printed on acid-free paper

For my beautiful wife, Katie. Without her hard work and patience with me, this book would not have been possible. I love you!

Table of Contents

For quick info about a recipe, look for these icons throughout the book:

Kitchen friendly
These recipes can be made using a normal kitchen stove.

Campfire approved
These recipes work best when cooked with charcoal briquettes in an outdoor setting.

Introduction

It's one of those priceless evenings in the wilderness. I sit in camp physically exhausted from the day's activities, yet all my senses are at an all-time high. There is a gentle mountain breeze stirring the incense of sage, aspen, and pine around the camp. Somewhere in the distance an annoyed squirrel chatters at a passerby. The lengthening rays of sun seem to intensify the colors of the mountains. The constant burbling of the small mountain stream gives a feeling of serenity to the scene. The wisps of smoke curling from the cook-fire reach my nose, adding the perfect spice to the evening. I lift the heavy lid of the Dutch oven and am immediately met by an aromatic puff of steam coming from the exquisite meal that I have prepared.

There are no words to describe the tastes of food prepared in this way; it's like a symphony of perfectly balanced flavors. There is something magical about Dutch-oven prepared food. It began as a necessity and has become a pleasurable pastime. Dutch ovens have been around as long as our country. Large, heavy cast iron cauldrons once graced the fireplace in many homes, constantly bubbling stocks and soups. Heavy-lidded, three-legged pots—staples for the pioneers trekking west across the plains—followed the cauldrons. Nowadays, Dutch ovens are coming out of attics, being dusted off and discovered anew. Whether it is to reconnect with our past or to add flare to the world of humdrum commercially prepared foods, I don't know. In places like Utah, Dutch ovens never died. What was a mainstay for the Mormon pioneers has stayed with the culture here.

Nowadays, Dutch ovens are coming out of attics, being dusted off and discovered anew.

Dutch oven cooking is one of the fastest growing hobbies among outdoor enthusiasts. Attracting thousands of newcomers every year, it has become a mainstay in the outdoor world. Yet it is surprising how very little is known about Dutch ovens and Dutch oven cooking. *Cast Iron Chef* was written to help readers understand Dutch ovens and to share cooking tips and recipes that will increase your confidence as you use a Dutch oven to make delicious and unconventional meals.

The word Dutch oven in and of itself is a misnomer; it is neither Dutch nor an oven. Yet simply say the word *Dutch oven*, and immediately people's minds will wander to a campsite with awesome potato-and-meat dishes that were prepared in a Dutch oven. The flavor of something cooked in a Dutch oven is not something

Is it the outdoor experience that makes the food so special, or is there really a secret to a Dutch oven that gives the food its flavor?

that can be imitated in any other type of cooking. The meat always seems to be tender and moist; the beans and potatoes are always great. The smoke from the cook-fire is a perfect spice for the food, blending in with the fresh mountain breeze. Is it the outdoor experience that makes the food so special, or is there really a secret to a Dutch oven that gives the food its flavor? How does a Dutch oven–cooked dish compare to a Crock Pot dish? How does a Dutch oven work? Can you cook healthy meals in a Dutch oven? Are Dutch ovens hard to care for? These are all questions I will answer in this book.

I have been exposed to Dutch oven cooking all of my life. It was a part of the culture where I grew up, a small town in central Utah that was settled in the mid 1800s. Brigham Young sent the original Mormon settlers to farm and develop the land. The pioneers had used Dutch Ovens extensively while crossing the plains to Utah, and they had brought the Dutch ovens with them as they established their new home. Their cooking secrets have been passed down through generations.

The idea behind the heavy, cast-iron pans was to cook food slowly and evenly with little or no maintenance. The pioneers, while breaking camp in the morning, would simply fill the heavy pans with water, potatoes, onions, meat, and whatever else and set them in a tin basin to ride in the wagon. Ashes from the morning cook-fire were shoveled into the basin. The dinner would cook all day at low temperatures in a very controlled environment with no fear of the meal burning. When the pioneers would stop to set up camp in the evening, dinner would be ready for the weary group.

Growing up with this heritage scattered throughout the town, I don't recall a single camping or social event where there wasn't a Dutch oven dish. From barbecued beans to Dutch oven potatoes, there was always a feast. Dutch oven cooking has always been big in Utah because of this heritage; in fact the International Dutch Oven Society is based in Utah and so are the World Championship Cook-offs. Vitually any kind of dish can be cooked in a Dutch oven, whether you are cooking a hearty breakfast, gooey sweetbread, or a chocolatey dessert.

Over the years, I have spent countless days cooking with my Dutch oven in the mountains, in my home, while catering parties, and for any other excuse I could find. So many people have come up to me and asked where I learned to cook these wonderful dishes. Many have complained about experiences they've had with cleaning or maintaining a Dutch oven and ask how I do it. Many others have complained about the lack of healthy recipes for Dutch ovens. I have had so many questions that I decided to write this book to help people understand more about Dutch ovens. Once you learn these techniques, you will find that great tasting and healthy Dutch oven cooking is possible, the ovens are easy to clean and care for, and you will have people asking where you found these great recipes when you prepare a dish for them.

Frequently Asked Questions

Think of a Dutch oven as a sort of an antique Crock Pot, a device made to cook the food slowly and evenly. Dutch ovens range in size from a small saucepan to a very large kettle. The most common sizes are between eight and twenty-two inches in diameter. Most Dutch ovens are made from cast iron, although there are a few cast aluminum Dutch ovens available on the market today. Generally speaking, a Dutch oven is a heavy metal casserole dish with a heavy, tight-fitting lid.

What kind of Dutch oven is best for me? Dutch ovens come in several varieties: some are made to be set on coals, others made to hang over a fire on a tripod, and others are made to sit on a stovetop or fire grate. Which style you choose should be determined by what activities you plan use it for. If you plan to take it camping a lot, the standard Dutch oven will suit you well. It is designed with three legs to allow coals to be placed underneath it to cook the food. The legs also allow the Dutch ovens to stack up with coals in between them to utilize more cooking for the amount of coals. Dutch ovens are available for purchase all over the United States. Anywhere you can find camping supplies, you can find a Dutch oven.

What size Dutch oven should I buy? That depends on how many people you are serving. I have used my twelve-quart Dutch oven for my family of five for a number of years just fine. I believe that the twelve-quart is the best all-around size for anyone to start with. If you really get into the hobby, you can purchase others in different sizes to have an array of dishes cooking at once.

Should I buy a traditional cast iron or a cast aluminum? I definitely recommend a cast iron for many reasons that will be discussed later in the book. The only time that I would recommend aluminum over cast iron is for groups that need to carry their supplies. This is because aluminum is a quarter the weight of a cast iron Dutch oven.

Should I buy a pre-seasoned oven or a regular Dutch oven? That depends on your budget. I recently competed in a Dutch oven chili cook-off where we were not allowed to bring our own pans. The Dutch ovens were provided for us new in the box to promote the sponsor of the cook-off. I was apprehensive at first because I am very particular about my Dutch ovens. The Dutch oven provided was a pre-seasoned Lewis and Clark edition Dutch oven made by Camp Chef. I was very surprised and pleased on how well it worked right out of the box. The only downfall of the pre-seasoned Dutch oven is it costs about 20–25 percent more than a conventional Dutch oven. A lot of companies have recently caught on to this trend and have been selling pre-seasoned Dutch ovens, but buyer beware, some are not very well seasoned and may have issues right out of the gate. Camp Chef has put out a "true seasoned" pre-seasoned Dutch oven that is remarkable. It would be a great oven for any beginner to pick up and learn with.

How much should I expect to spend on a Dutch oven? Anywhere from twenty to eighty is about right, any less (other than ones you find secondhand) will not be a quality made oven, and anything over that price is simply an overpriced gimmick and should be avoided, unless you like that particular gimmick. An example would be an oven with the lid cast in a fancy pattern, name, or event. It won't affect the way the oven cooks at all but will cost a lot more. When you are looking at a Dutch oven, look for three things:

1. Make sure the lid fits well on the Dutch oven. Any large gaps or a loose fitting lid and the Dutch oven will never cook properly and should be avoided. You should be able to freely turn the lid on the Dutch oven, but you should not be able to slide it back and forth.

2. Look for an oven with a solid handle on top of the lid. This is a necessity, since you will lift the lid a lot during the cooking process.

3. Make sure the legs are long enough to allow standard-size charcoal briquettes to fit underneath. If the legs are too short, you will fight your Dutch oven every time you use it.

You may be able to find a secondhand Dutch oven stored away in your grandpa's attic or at a garage sale. Some of these old relics can be the very best to use if they were treated correctly since a Dutch oven gets better with every use. The only drawback is if it has been mistreated. Rust spots can *Whatever Dutch oven you choose, it will be a lifelong, valuable tool if it is used correctly.* ruin the metal and cause hot spots in the Dutch oven. The metal may be cracked or warped from misuse, resulting in very poor performance. The best thing to do is to inspect the Dutch oven carefully before you buy it. The Dutch oven should have a dark brown or black color throughout. Inspect it carefully for warps, cracks, or deep rust pockets. If you find any of these things, the oven should be avoided. Don't be afraid of a small amount of rust (you should be able to wipe it away with your fingers or a rag). This happens over time if oil is applied often and breaks down. Also, don't be afraid of a slightly rancid oil smell. That happens if it was oiled heavily and left for a long period of time.

This is easily remedied by cleaning out the old oil and re-seasoning the Dutch oven.

Whatever Dutch oven you choose, it will be a lifelong, valuable tool if it is used correctly. Some of the best meals you will ever eat will be cooked with your Dutch oven. The only drawback to owning a Dutch oven for the outdoor enthusiast is the weight, making it improbable to backpack with. But with that exception, they are the most valuable and versatile camping tools you can own.

Seasoning Your Dutch Oven

Season. This is that big bad word that scares most people away from Dutch ovens, yet it is so simple to do. If you are lucky you will only have to do this once with your oven, or if you buy a pre-seasoned Dutch oven, never. Seasoning is misunderstood, but very simple. To understand what a season is, it is important to understand the nature of cast iron. Cast iron is a fairly porous metal when viewed from a microscope. There are millions of ridges and pockets between the iron particles. Seasoning a Dutch oven is simply filling those pockets and ridges with oil. Sounds simple enough, doesn't it? It is. The challenge with a seasoned Dutch oven is getting that oil to stay there. If your Dutch oven is not seasoned, anything you try to cook will fill in those pockets and ridges, causing it to stick terribly and frustrate the cook to no end.

How do I season a Dutch oven? The first thing you need to do is clean out all the packing wax or grease from the manufacturer. With the exception of the pre-seasoned Dutch ovens, all the Dutch ovens will come coated with wax or grease. This is to prevent the cast iron from rusting, because you wouldn't want to buy a rusty old Dutch oven, would you? There is a lot of debate among the experts on how to properly remove this coating. Some will burn their Dutch ovens, while others will *Seasoning is misunderstood, but very simple.* scour it in the sink with a strong detergent. There really is no right or wrong way as long as you get it all out. My personal preference is the dishwasher. This is the one and only time I will ever let my Dutch oven even come close to a dishwasher. The hot water and detergent do a good job of getting rid of the grease.

How do you tell when all the packaging grease is off? All you have to do is let it sit for a few hours after you've cleaned it. If the grease is off, the Dutch oven will have a light coat of rust on it. The rust is a good thing at this point because you know that the grease is gone. If it is not a little rusty, re-wash it and try it again. This can also be used to re-season an old or abused Dutch oven. The Dutch oven has to be absolutely clear for the seasoning to work. One of the best Dutch ovens I own, I washed in the dishwasher and set it outside in a rainstorm (accidentally). I returned the next day to find an orange Dutch oven. I cleaned it well and seasoned it, and it has been my favorite Dutch oven since. I am not saying to abuse your pans badly, as too much stress can cause damage that cannot be fixed. However, the more you can do at this point to clean it, the better the season will take to your Dutch oven.

What do I do once the packaging grease is all off? Now you are ready to season the Dutch oven. To do this, heat up your Dutch oven in a fire, stove, or oven for a few minutes at high heat. This will open up the pores and allow your oil to get in deep. When the Dutch oven is heated up, with a leather glove and a clean rag wipe in some oil or shortening (I prefer canola oil because it is healthier and doesn't break down easily) until the Dutch oven won't take any more and appears oily. Place the Dutch oven back in the oven or above a cool fire (about 300–350 degrees) upside down and keep it there for at least thirty minutes. If you do not place the oven upside down, you will not season your oven at all; all you will do is cause an oil slick to appear on the top of your oven. The reason is that as the oil gets hot, it vaporizes and begins to rise. The open pores of the cast iron will allow the vaporized oil to fill them, creating the season. You only need to season the inside, or cooking surface of your cast iron. You should expect some smoke and an odd oily, hot metal smell, so when I do this I open the windows and keep a fan on. Because of this, a lot of people season their Dutch ovens outside on their barbecue grills. This will work just as well. Just turn the heat to medium, since you don't want the oil to burn, just vaporize. Trust me, it will be worth the smell and the effort in the end. When you have finished this process, let the Dutch oven cool to room temperature, wipe off any excess oil, and re-apply a light coat of oil. Your Dutch oven is now seasoned and ready for use.

Patina: the dark brown or black layer that you see in a well-used Dutch oven. Essentially, patina is carbon that has built up and adhered to the metal.

The seasoning on your Dutch oven at this point is fragile, however, and must be treated right for it to stay there. You will need to build up a layer of *patina* to seal in the oil and create the ultimate cooking machine. Patina is the dark brown or black layer that you see in a well-used Dutch oven. Essentially, patina is carbon that has built up and adhered to the metal.

Patina builds up every time you use the Dutch oven. The more a Dutch oven is used, the more the patina builds up and the better it cooks. As it builds

Most people know not to scrub out their Dutch oven with a strong dish detergent, but almost everyone puts their Dutch oven away for weeks or months, with a heavy coat of oil in it.

up, the patina creates a smooth non-stick layer that is better than Teflon any day without any of the harmful side effects. The more patina you have, the better your Dutch oven will cook and the easier it will be to clean.

Patina has its enemies: steel wool, wire brushes, dishwashing detergent, and rancid oil. All these things will break it down and leave your oven vulnerable. The oil takes its toll on more Dutch ovens than all the rest. Most people know not to scrub out their Dutch oven with a wire brush or steel wool, and most people have heard of the ill effects of using a strong dish detergent. Almost everyone, though, puts their Dutch oven away for weeks or months with a heavy coat of oil in it. They almost always open the lid to the smell of rancid oil and small black flakes in the Dutch oven. This is because the oil goes rancid and starts to break down the Patina. Your Dutch oven will never perform well like this; food will always stick and the flavor will always be off. When you store your Dutch oven, you should never coat it with a lot of oil. See page 17 for proper storage techniques.

The Science of Dutch Oven Cooking

Understanding how a Dutch oven works will help you to cook well, clean easily, and care for your Dutch oven properly. To understand how a Dutch oven works, it is important to understand how it is made. Most Dutch ovens are made of porous cast iron. As discussed in the previous chapter, filling the pits and ridges in metal with oil is called seasoning the Dutch oven. Understanding how the seasoning works requires a basic knowledge of some simple cooking principles.

The first principle is called heat transfer. Heat transfer is simply the exchange of heat from the heat source into the food you are trying to cook. Heat transfer is accomplished through one of three principles: convection, conduction, and radiation. Conduction is the most common transfer in cooking. The heat from the heat source, a stovetop for example, heats up a pan that then conducts the heat into the food source. Convection uses the movement of hot air to heat up the food source, much like baking something in an oven. Radiation transfers heat in waves that produce friction. Radiant heat is more commonly known as microwaves. Microwaves tranfer

Heat transfer is simply the exchange of heat from the heat source into the food you are trying to cook.

heat by transmitting thousands of concentrated radio waves. This produces friction that in turn produces heat as it passes through the food source. The unique characteristic of a Dutch oven is that it uses all three of the heat transfer mediums to cook your food.

First let's talk about conduction. At one point or another, most people have cooked with a pan that had "hot spots." These are especially prevalent in stainless steel cookware. This is because stainless steel is a very poor conductor of heat. The molecules in the stainless steel are so tightly bonded together that the heat does not dissipate throughout the pan. This can be seen often, as you can see by the rings of an electric stove or gas marks from your gas stove on the cooking surface of your pan. Conduction works best through a fluid medium. That is why deep fat frying is the very best way to cook something evenly, though definitely not the healthiest. The oil, when frying, is all at the same temperature. Any fluid will be a great heat conductor, but as with the case of a water-based fluid, it quickly evaporates after reaching a meager 200 degrees. The more solid the molecules in a surface are, the worse it conducts heat. This is why properly seasoned cast iron cookware is the best heat-conducting cookware available. The pockets that I discussed earlier, now filled with oil after being seasoned, create a fluid conduction in your Dutch oven. As the heat source heats up, the oil molecules in the Dutch oven span the gaps in the cast iron molecules and heat the Dutch oven up very evenly, giving you very little, or no, "hot spots." This creates almost a perfect conduction-cooking atmosphere, cooking your food evenly. The patina I talked about earlier seals the oil into these pockets, solidifying your seasoning in your Dutch oven. Therefore, the more you cook with your cast iron pans, the more durable and heat conductive they become.

A Dutch oven is an all-purpose tool, able to fry a steak, roast a chicken, and even bake a loaf of bread with very little effort.

The Dutch oven's ability to cook with convection heat transfer is probably why it's called an oven. This ability is also what sets it apart from Crock Pots and other slow cookers. There is no way you could cook a bread dish in a crock-pot, yet Dutch oven bread recipes abound. The Dutch oven can cook with convection because of its shape and its heavy lid. Dutch ovens are built with very heavy walls and lids so that the heat inside the oven has nowhere to go. The steam and heat waves circulate, cooking the food from all sides very evenly. If you open your Dutch oven while it's cooking, just like your oven at home, you will instantly lose the convection and it will take a little time to build back up again. That is why I recommend that you know your approximate cooking times and not open the Dutch oven until that time is up to avoid losing this valuable cooking tool. Convection heat transfer will not work in an overfull Dutch oven, since the gases and heat waves will not be allowed to circulate properly. I never recommend filling your Dutch oven more than two-thirds of the way full if you want to take advantage of the convective heat.

Radiant heat is very easy to understand. If you have ever sat out in the sun on a summer morning and felt the rays of sunshine warm your body, then you have experienced radiant heat transfer. Radiant heat transfer occurs when the waves of heat pass through an object, causing friction, which then heats up the object. If you have ever cooked on a grill, then you know that the heat waves are forced upwards from the heat source, cooking the food. Inside of your Dutch oven, the heat that accumulates from the conduction rises upward and, as I said before, because of the thick walls and lid, has nowhere to go. The friction of these heat waves rising causes the food to heat up. Also, long after the Dutch oven has been removed from the heat source, the radiant heat of the heat-conducted Dutch oven will continue to cook the food for quite some time. This is sometimes referred to as residual heat.

The Dutch oven's ability to utilize all three types of heat transfer is what makes it unique. It's an all-purpose tool, able to fry a steak, roast a chicken, and even bake a loaf of bread with very little effort. The Dutch oven can also be used anywhere with almost any heat source. I cook just as much at home with my Dutch oven as I do in the mountains. I use it in my oven at home as well as on my stovetop. I use it while camping, using coals from the campfire and using charcoal briquettes when I am competing in a Dutch oven cook-off.

Cleaning Your Dutch Oven

Proper cleaning of a Dutch oven has been debated by many and understood by few. Some will tell you to turn your Dutch oven upside down in a fire and burn the food out. Some swear by soap while others refuse to allow it to touch their Dutch ovens. Many experts just wipe it clean and oil it. Which is right? Let's talk about the science of your Dutch oven, then I'll tell you how I clean mine, and you can decide for yourself.

First of all, the more you can maintain your season and build up the patina, the better your Dutch oven will cook. In my thinking, if you burn a Dutch oven in a fire, you are not only burning out the food but also the oil or season in your Dutch oven. I will only burn out a Dutch oven for one reason: if the oven has been ruined and I need to start the seasoning process all over again. In terms of preserving the seasoning in your Dutch oven, what do you think using soap in your Dutch oven does to that important oil? When the Exxon Valdez dumped thousands of gallons of oil into the ocean, the cleanup volunteers used Dawn dish detergent to break down the oil on the oil-covered animals. Soap, especially dish detergent, is specifically designed to break down oils to wash your dishes. If you are trying to preserve the oil in your Dutch oven, dish detergent is definitely the wrong approach; you will need to re-season almost every time. But don't worry if you accidentally drop a little soap in your Dutch oven. I'm only talking about scrubbing it with a lot of detergent. The only exception to this rule is a well-used Dutch oven with a good buildup of patina. A little soap will not affect the oil much at all since the patina protects it. As for my recommendations, I try and stay away from soap as much as possible.

Wiping the oven out with a paper towel and then applying oil works well for maintaining a season, but what happens if you cook a cobbler or something a little sticky? There is no way to effectively get all of it out in this manner, and then you've got yourself a beautiful bacteria culture that any biology teacher would be proud to view under a microscope. So, how do you clean it out effectively while building up patina and maintaining a season? Think back to the pioneer times.

How would the pioneers have cleaned a Dutch oven on the trail? Soap, if available, would have been mild lye and lard soap, definitely not a detergent. Simply scrubbing it out with a boar bristle brush and water cleaned the Dutch ovens. I use this same technique with great results every time I use my Dutch oven. I have a plastic (not boar bristle) scrub brush that I use, rinsing often with water.

When the Dutch oven is clean, I wipe it out with a paper towel and let it dry upside down for a couple of minutes. I then apply a light coat of oil before putting the Dutch oven away. It is as simple as that. My Dutch ovens take almost no effort to clean, even after cooking a cobbler. However you decide to clean your Dutch oven, just remember to preserve the season and build up patina, and you will be all right. The number one sin in cleaning a Dutch oven is using a dishwasher. Don't do it, no matter how much you are tempted. It will destroy your Dutch oven!

Storage & Maintenance

Storing and maintaining your Dutch oven is one area most people think that they understand and do well. Unfortunately, this is the area where most people need the most help. Too many times, I've seen people open a Dutch oven's lid and nearly be knocked out by the stench of rancid oil. They rinse it out, re-oil it, and then wonder why their Dutch oven does not perform well. Everything they cook seems to stick, the Dutch oven seems to have "hot spots," and when they clean it they notice gray streaks in the bottom of what should be a uniform charcoal-black Dutch oven. This problem is caused by not storing the Dutch oven properly.

There is a single bad technique for storage that 90 percent of people with Dutch ovens use. Because so few people use their Dutch ovens on a regular basis, it may sit for six to nine months between uses. Because the time between uses is so long, they will heavily coat their Dutch oven with oil inside and out and set it in their garage or storage shed until its next emergence. I don't know where this practice originated, but I can understand the reasoning behind it. Most people see cast iron as an unstable metal that can rust easily, which is true. People believe that coating the Dutch oven with oil will stave off the rust. This would work great if you used motor oil or some other petroleum-based product. (The obvious problem with this would be the flavor in your food.) The food oil that most people slather on is unstable and breaks down quickly. What happens is that the oil breaks down and becomes rancid. As it does so, it becomes caustic and goes to work breaking down the patina or protective layer in your Dutch oven.

As the patina breaks down, the seasoning in your Dutch oven falls under attack and becomes rancid as well. So when you go to use your Dutch oven, three things will happen: (1) your food will take on a rancid oil taste; (2) because the seasoning in your Dutch oven will be mostly or all gone, the natural capillary action of the porous cast iron will try to fill the voids with whatever it can (whatever you are cooking), causing a lot of food to stick; (3) because your Dutch oven filled those voids with what you cooked, the next time you cook a peach cobbler, it will taste a little like the lasagna you cooked previously. Yuck!

Now, I know what you are thinking, Well, how do I keep the Dutch oven from rusting?

The best way to store your Dutch oven is to store it as it is. Just make sure that the Dutch oven is completely dry before you store it. The seasoning and the patina on your Dutch oven are all you need to keep the rust off. That, and storing your Dutch oven in a dry place. When you pull out your Dutch oven to use it, wipe it down with a little oil before you use it, that's all. A lot of people go through a process of oiling their Dutch oven every time they use it. That is simply not necessary. Again, I wipe my Dutch oven with oil before I use it, not after. The only other maintenance item on the checklist is re-seasoning your Dutch oven every couple of years. To do this, clean the oven thoroughly with warm water (no soap). Heat up the Dutch oven and wipe a small amount of oil on the cooking surfaces. Place the oven upside down in a 350-degree oven or on a grill at medium heat for ten minutes or so. Let the Dutch oven cool down, and then wipe out the excess oil. It's that simple.

The following list is a cleaning and storage schedule to properly maintain you Dutch oven. Follow these items and you'll never have any problems with your Dutch oven.

1. Before you cook, wipe down the cooking surfaces with canola oil, making sure they are clean.
2. After you cook:
   a. Clean the Dutch oven as soon as possible.
   b. Use water and a plastic scrub brush to remove all the food and residue. (Note: if you use warm water or the Dutch oven is still warm, it will be easier to clean.)
   c. Never, never burn your Dutch oven out or use salt to clean it. You will damage your oven.
   d. When cleaning an oven after you've cooked a dessert or something sugary, use hot water to remove the residue, it will come right off. Do not scrape it!

e. Wipe out the oven with paper towels to dry it as much as possible.

f. Let the Dutch oven air-dry with the lid off, or heat both up slightly until the moisture is completely gone.

g. Close the lid and store in a cool, dry place. If you have a Dutch oven bag, use it.

h. Don't ever oil your Dutch oven before storing. It takes only a few weeks to go rancid, and it will damage your Dutch oven.

i. If your Dutch oven gets a little rust on it, don't despair. Simply scrub it with a scrub brush and water, warm the Dutch oven up to dry it, and wipe it down with oil before you cook with it.

j. Remember, the more you use your Dutch oven, the easier it is to clean and store.

Dutch Oven Secrets

Most people only think of a Dutch oven as a slow cooker. There is so much more to it though. There are four methods of cooking with a Dutch oven, each with a different application. In the recipe section, I will specify which application will work best for each recipe.

1. Roasting
2. Broasting
3. Baking
4. Broiling

1. Roasting

This is the most common method for cooking in a Dutch oven. Roasting simply means all the heat is coming from the bottom of the Dutch oven. Traditionally this was the most common method. People would place their Dutch oven directly on coals from a fire or hang their Dutch oven from a tripod over an open fire. In modern times, I cook with my Dutch oven in my kitchen, using my stovetop. While camping, I frequently roast dinners on my Camp Chef 30,000 BTU burner. Roasting is best suited for soup, stews, and frying.

2. Broasting

Broasting is the absolute best way to cook any whole meat, such as a roast. Broasting means that most of the heat is on the bottom with a little heat on the top. The effect of broasting is that the meat will caramelize on the top without becoming dried out. An example of broasting would be twenty charcoal briquettes on the bottom of your oven and ten charcoal briquettes on top. Broasting produces superior meat dishes that are nicely caramelized and not overdone. The disadvantage is you have to be outside to do it. A lot of the recipes for meat dishes in this book will give you the option of broasting or roasting. The rule of thumb for broasting is to have half the amount of heat on the top as you do the bottom. If you are using briquettes, that is an easy equation. If you are using coals from a fire, just guess as close as you can. There is not an exact science to it.

3. Baking

Baking is what most people do all the time with their Dutch ovens. Baking is simply equal heat on top and bottom. To achieve true baking, you need slightly more coals on the top because heat rises, so it takes more to achieve balanced heat. The only time I bake in a Dutch oven is for breads and desserts that I need a full convection of heat. I very rarely use baking for meat dishes since they have a tendency to overcook, leaving them dry. Baking in your Dutch oven is easy at home. Simply place it inside your conventional oven, adding 25 degrees to the temperature called for in the recipe.

4. Broiling

Broiling is the least used method in Dutch oven cooking. I use broiling a lot of times as a finishing stage on a dish rather than a whole process. Broiling means that all the heat is on the top of the Dutch oven. Remember, heat rises, so if you are trying to broil at a certain temperature, you need to use more coals than you would to achieve the same temperature on the bottom. Broiling works excellent for dishes in which you want a heavy caramelizing on the top. I will use it a lot for dishes with a sugar glaze or cheese on top for the last part of the process to finish off a dish.

Secret #1: Use charcoal briquettes to reach the desired temperature.

My own feelings are that people spend way too much time worrying about the coals, especially since individual briquettes vary greatly in the amount of heat they produce. A good rule of thumb is that two briquettes on the bottom equal approximately twenty-five degrees in your Dutch oven, while three briquettes on the top equal twenty-five degrees. Watch for the amount of steam coming out from the lid. If the steam is coming out in billows, it's too hot, so take off a couple of briquettes. Most of the time, I like to cook between 250–350 degrees. At that temperature, you should see some steam, but it will be gentle. Just keep cooking with your Dutch oven, and you'll get a better feel for using it. The saying "practice makes perfect" definitely applies in Dutch oven cooking.

Secret #2: Use the right oil in the right way.

I almost always use a little oil in the bottom of the Dutch oven when I cook. You don't need a lot, a capful will usually work. The oil helps to balance the heat transfer from the Dutch oven into your food. Don't just use any oil; I like to use canola oil for two reasons: (1) it is a very stable cooking oil; and (2) it is a monounsaturated fat, meaning it is healthy for you, rather than harmful like a lot of other oils.

In most of the recipes it says to heat a little oil in your Dutch oven. Basically all that is needed is just enough to make the Dutch oven glossy. Resist any temptation you may have to use spray oil like Pam, even if it is canola. These light spritz-type oils may work great on your Teflon at home, but they are not stable enough to last cooking in a Dutch oven.

Secret #3: Use the right kind of onions.

Most people think that an onion is an onion and that recipes that use onions just need an onion thrown in. Onions are the number one spice used worldwide in almost any cuisine. There are several varieties of onions with a broad flavor range. Basically, you can classify all onions into two groups: sharp or sweet. Sharp onions are generally young with the starches mostly still intact. Think of them like a piece of fruit that is not yet ripe, the flavor will always be stronger. Use a sharp onion in recipes where you want the onion to be a strong flavor. The easiest way to tell a sharp onion from a sweet onion is that a sharp onion is longer that it is wide. That is because it has not reached full maturity. Your common everyday yellow onions are almost always sharp.

Sweet onions are fully ripe onions of varieties that remain tender as they ripen. Sweet onions have most of the starches converted to sugars. You should use sweet onions in recipes where you want the onion flavor to be complementary rather than dominant. Sweet onions are easy to distinguish because they are wider than they are long. A lot of your specialty onions are the sweet variety, such as New Mexico sweets, Walla Walla, and Bermuda. In all of my recipes, I will specify whether to use a sharp or a sweet onion.

The only other types of onions I use in the following recipes are green onions. Green onions are simply the plant or leaves of the onion.

For these recipes, you can use chives, standard green onions, or leeks. Experiment and find what you like the best.

The most important tip I have for onions is that they need to be carmelized or browned in order to release the flavor into the dish. If you do not do this, your dish will take on little of the flavor and the onions themselves will be very potent. To caramelize the onions, heat them by themselves or with the meat and stir-fry them until they are clear. When they become transparent, you can tell that the starches have all converted to sugars and the flavor is being released into your dish. The further you cook your onions, the more their profile will change. Some recipes will call for browned onions rather than carmelized. The browned onions will have been further cooked, and instead of being transparent, they will be slightly brown. Browned onions take on a sweet, nutty taste. Take the time to experiment and have fun using the champion of spices.

Secret #4: Learn to use starches to properly thicken your sauces.

Flour is the most common starch used to thicken a sauce, but it has its drawbacks. If you just stir flour into your sauce, most of the time it will thicken but will leave your sauce with lumps. The reason for this is that the flour gluten binds together before it has a chance to dissipate into the sauce. The way to combat this problem is to create a *roux*. A roux (pronounced "ru") is simply flour mixed with oil. The oil separates the flour molecules, preventing them from binding before they have an opportunity to dissipate into your sauce and thicken it. Rouxs come in various forms with different flavors and thickening abilities. The three used in this book are blonde roux, brown roux, and brick roux.

The blonde roux will thicken the best but adds little or no flavor. The blonde roux is the basis of most French cooking. To create a blonde roux, heat equal amounts of oil and flour, whisking vigorously over medium heat until the roux is blonde to golden in color. A blonde roux can be kept tightly covered in your fridge for last minute use. I use the blonde roux for most soups and delicate sauces in which I don't want the flavor of a roux to interfere with the sauce profile.

The brown roux will not thicken as well as the blonde but adds a hint of a nutty flavor to your dish. This is because the cereals in your flour have actually started to cook, giving it a nice flavor. I will use a brown roux any time I am thickening gravy with a whole meat, such as a roast. To create a brown roux, start out just like you were making a blonde and continue to whisk and cook until it is milk chocolate in color.

The brick roux has very little thickening power compared to the other two but has a very strong, unique flavor that is a basis for Cajun cooking. I usually only use a brick roux for Cajun cooking, so I make it as I need it because it may not store for the amount of time between cooking Cajun-type meals. To create a brick roux, begin the same way you would the others. Just continue whisking over medium heat until it is the color of an old red brick. This will take upwards of twenty to forty minutes and requires near constant attention to keep it from burning, becoming no good to anybody (especially the person who has to clean the Dutch oven). The brick roux may take some practice to get right, but the Dutch oven makes it easy to do, compared to other pans.

The second most used starch, and definitely the easiest, is cornstarch. To use cornstarch, mix it in equal portions with water and pour it into your sauce until you achieve the desired thickness. The most important thing is to be sure the sauce is at a boiling point, or the starch won't work. This is why, if you choose to use cornstarch with a recipe that calls for cream, you need to over-thicken with the starch and stir in the cream later, because boiling the cream will change the flavor and texture of your sauce. The other advantage of cornstarch is that it has no taste at all and is perfect for delicate sauces. I use cornstarch most of the time because of its simplicity to use and its lack of flavor.

Though almost any starch will work to thicken a sauce, there is just one more I want to mention. Arrowroot can be found at almost any health food store. It works much the same way as cornstarch but produces an extremely silky, light texture to your sauce. The drawback is the price. It is ten times (sometimes more) the cost of cornstarch and therefore not worth the price most of the time, unless I am really setting out to impress.

In the recipes, I simply indicate to thicken with a starch, unless it is a dish that needs a particular roux. This way you can use whichever starch you are the most comfortable with. Feel free to experiment and try out different styles and thicknesses to find what you like the best.

Secret #5: Keep the liquid level low.

Most people treat their Dutch oven like a Crock Pot, filling it to the top with water. This if fine if you are making a soup, but it ruins meat. For meat to keep its flavor and texture, you need to keep the liquid level at one-third of the way up the meat. This will allow the fats and juices that will naturally draw out from the meat to caramelize and form a crust of sorts to protect the integrity of the meat. When you fill the Dutch oven full of liquid, you end up boiling the meat, leaving it dry and bland. Keeping the liquid level low will vastly improve the quality of your meat, but it does take a little extra time to check the meat to make sure it doesn't burn.

Secret #6: Use your Dutch oven often and have fun.

The more you cook, the better you'll get, and the better your Dutch oven will perform. Dutch oven cooking is a fun hobby that will bring you the admiration of all who try your cooking.

Beef Recipes

This is a selection of some of my favorite beef recipes. Unless I specify a particular type or cut of beef, any will do. If you want a lower-fat dish, use a cut from the round or the sirloin. The shoulder and rib roasts have a lot more fat, but they also have more flavor.

Basic Roast
Sticky Beef
Swiss Steaks
Cheese Steak
Matt's Sirloin Tips
Swedish Meatballs
Steak & Everything
Grandma's Pot Roast
Island Teriyaki Roast
Rosemary Sirloin Roast

Basic Roast

This is the basic Sunday dinner roast, enjoyed by people around the world. I feel it is best suited for the Dutch oven, as you get the best results from broasting

> 1 (2–3 lb.) lean roast, such as a round or sirloin
> 1 large sharp onion
> 1 (14 oz.) can beef broth or stock, or 2 beef bouillon
>   cubes in 2 c. water
> 1 bay leaf
> 1 pinch nutmeg
> 1 tsp. black pepper
> salt to taste
> 3 Tbsp. cold water
> 3 Tbsp. cornstarch

Heat just enough oil to make the bottom of your Dutch oven glossy. Brown the roast on all sides. Remove the roast from the oven and set aside. Stir-fry the onion in the remaining oil until the onion is clear. Add the beef broth to the onions and reduce the heat to about 250–300 degrees. Add the roast, bay leaf, nutmeg, black pepper, and salt to taste. Roast or broast for 3–5 hours. If broasting, rotate every 30 minutes. Keep the liquid level at one-third the way up the roast to allow the meat to caramelize. Mix the water and cornstarch. Remove the roast and add half the starch/water combo to the liquid left in the Dutch oven and increase the heat. Continue to add and stir in the starch mixture until the desired thickness is achieved. Cut the roast into cross-grain slices and add back to the gravy.

Tips:
1. **For darker gravy, allow the liquid to boil down before adding water and starch—the lower, the darker.**
2. **If you do not want to mix the meat in the gravy, remove some liquid from the pot and pour it over the cut meat. Without liquid, the meat will dry out.**

Sticky Beef

This is a simple honey-barbecued beef that goes well with Dutch oven potatoes or with Dutch oven rolls. It is best served with corn.

2–3 lbs. beef, cut into strips
1 (14 oz.) can beef broth
¼ c. honey
juice and ½ tsp. zest from 1 orange
1 c. barbecue sauce

Lightly brown the beef in the Dutch oven. Add the beef broth, honey, orange juice, and zest. Simmer for 90 minutes or until tender. Add water as needed. Stir in the barbecue sauce and cook 5–10 minutes more.

Swiss Steaks

The secret to this recipe is that the steaks cook for a long time at a low temperature. This recipe has Swiss origins, although I'm uncertain how directly the recipe ties in to old-time recipes. This makes a great formal family dinner. I like to serve it over boiled potato chunks.

I large sharp onion
I tsp. butter
I lb. breakfast sausage links
2 lbs. beef steaks (any type)
I can (14.5 oz.) crushed tomatoes
2 bay leaves
2 tsp. oregano
I c. apple juice
5 Tbsp. honey
2 cubes chicken bouillon

Heat conventional oven to 250 degrees or use charcoals to establish that temperature in your Dutch oven. Cut onions into rings, then caramelize in skillet with butter. Remove onions from skillet and set aside. Cut sausage links into bite-sized chunks, and brown in a skillet. Remove from skillet and set aside. Lightly brown steaks on both sides in a skillet with hot oil and set aside. In the Dutch oven, combine all ingredients and cook on low heat for 3 hours. Watch this dish closely and add water if sauce becomes too low and starts to burn. When you are ready to serve this meal, the sauce should be thick and soup-like in consistency.

Cheese Steak

A family favorite, this can be served on bread as a sandwich, with potatoes, or with rice. It goes well with a pepper medley or another green vegetable.

1 small sweet onion, chopped
2 lbs. beef, sliced thin
salt to taste
1 tsp. coarse black pepper
juice from ½ lemon
¼ lb. sliced Swiss, provolone, or mozzarella cheese

Heat just enough oil to make the bottom of your Dutch oven glossy. Add the onion and fry until they are clear. Add the meat while the Dutch oven is hot. Stir-fry until the meat is beginning to brown. Add the remaining ingredients. Broast or roast for 15–20 minutes at a low temperature, 200–225 degrees. Layer cheese on top.

Matt's Sirloin Tips

This is one of my favorite Dutch oven recipes. It is best served over long grain rice with a green vegetable.

2 lbs. sirloin roast or steak, cut into strips
1 medium onion
4 Tbsp. flour
2 cloves garlic, minced
1 c. apple juice
1 c. Coca-Cola
2 Tbsp. butter
¼ c. Worcestershire sauce
1 beef bouillon cube
salt to taste
3 Tbsp. cornstarch (optional)
3 Tbsp. cold water (optional)

Heat just enough butter to make the bottom of your Dutch oven glossy. Add the onions and meat. Cook until the meat is browned; add the flour and stir it in with the meat. Add the remaining ingredients; simmer 90 minutes, adding liquid if necessary. The liquid should be gravy-like. If not, add cornstarch/water mixture and thicken at high heat. The meat should be very tender before serving.

Swedish Meatballs

I learned this recipe from a Swedish friend of mine, and it's my favorite way to prepare ground meat. It's easy and always popular. It is best served over rice or egg noodles.

I lb. ground beef
½ lb. ground pork sausage
4 cloves garlic, minced
I c. bread crumbs
salt to taste
2 eggs
I (10.5 oz.) can cream of mushroom soup
½ c. chopped mushrooms
I c. sour cream

Begin by mixing ground beef, sausage, garlic, bread crumbs, and salt together. Whip eggs until they are twice their original volume; stir eggs into meat mixture. Form into meatballs. Set meatballs in a Dutch oven and layer with mushroom soup, mushrooms, and sour cream. Bake at 400 degrees for 45 minutes. Let stand 5 minutes before serving.

Steak & Everything

The name of this one says it all. It is typically served as a sandwich but is a great main dish served with rice or potatoes.

1 medium sweet onion, chopped
2 lbs. thin-sliced beef
juice from ½ lemon
½ lb. sliced mushrooms
1 red or green bell pepper (I prefer red)
1 tsp. coarse black pepper
salt to taste
1 large tomato, cubed
¼ lb. Swiss, provolone, or mozzarella cheese

Heat just enough oil to make the bottom of your Dutch oven glossy. Stir your onions and meat until the meat begins to brown. Squeeze lemon juice over meat. Add the mushrooms, bell pepper, black pepper, and salt to taste. Cover and roast at low heat, 200–250 degrees, for 20–30 minutes. Add the tomatoes and cheese. Cook for 2–3 minutes.

 # Grandma's Pot Roast

As the name implies, this is a classic American pot roast. As such, it needs to be from a front-quarter cut, such as a blade or a chuck roast. It should be served with potatoes, gravy, and carrots.

2 Tbsp. butter
1 (2–3 lb.) chuck or blade roast
1 large sweet onion, chopped
1 c. apple juice
2 bay leaves
1 pinch ground cloves
salt to taste

Melt the butter in the bottom of your Dutch oven. Brown the roast and, at the same time, caramelize the onion. Add the remaining ingredients and bake or broast at 250–300 degrees for 2–3 hours. Check regularly for moisture and add water, thickening to a gravy. When ready to serve, the meat should be pulled and not cut.

Island Teriyaki Roast

As the name implies, this recipe is influenced by Pacific Island flavors. This meat works wonderfully for an outside meal and is ideal served with lots of fresh fruit. It also tastes delicious served over rice.

1 (2–3 lb.) beef roast
1 (20 oz.) can crushed pineapple
1 c. soy sauce
4 Tbsp. molasses
2 tsp. powdered ginger
3 Tbsp. brown sugar

Put all ingredients into the Dutch oven and roast or broast at 200 degrees for three hours. When done, pull meat apart with a fork and make sure that all meat is covered with sauce.

Rosemary Sirloin Roast

As the name says, this roast should be a sirloin. This dish goes well with Dutch oven red potatoes or wild rice and a green vegetable.

1 (2–3 lb.) sirloin roast
1 medium sharp onion
3 Tbsp. flour
3 cloves garlic, crushed
1 sprig fresh rosemary or 2 tsp. dry rosemary
5 Tbsp. brown sugar or honey
¼ c. Worcestershire sauce
2 Tbsp. soy sauce
2 tsp. crushed black peppercorns
1 (14 oz.) can beef broth or stock, or 2 beef bouillon
   cubes in 1 c. water

Heat just enough oil to make the bottom of your Dutch oven glossy. Brown the roast, remove from Dutch oven, and set aside. Slice the onion and stir-fry in the oil until the onions are clear. Add the flour and crushed garlic. Cook until garlic begins to brown. Add the roast and the remaining ingredients; roast or broast 3–5 hours, keeping the liquid one-third of the way up the roast. Remove the roast and half the liquid. Cut the roast cross-grain and return to the Dutch oven, or drizzle the liquid over the meat before serving.

Poultry Recipes

Dutch ovens work very well with poultry. I have rarely had a dry poultry dish prepared in a Dutch oven. This is a selection of some of my favorites. If you would like to have a lower-fat dish, remove the skin.

Margarita Chicken
Barbecued Tenders
Lemon Pepper Chicken
Honey Mustard Cutlets
Creamed Spinach Cutlets
Mesquite Barbecued Turkey
Chicken Cordon Bleu with Sauce

Margarita Chicken

This recipe is from the Pacific region of Mexico. This is great served with tortillas, rice, and fresh salsa.

3 lbs. boneless skinless chicken breasts
2 c. margarita mixer
juice from 1 lime
1 tsp. lime zest
2 Tbsp. brown sugar
1 poblano chile, chopped
1 large tomato, chopped
fresh cilantro to taste

Heat just enough oil to make the bottom of your Dutch oven glossy. Brown the chicken breasts on both sides. Add all the ingredients except the tomato and cilantro. Roast or broast for 30 minutes at 250–300 degrees. Add the tomato and cilantro and remove from heat. Let it stand 2–3 minutes. Cut the chicken into pieces or serve whole.

Barbecued Tenders

This is probably the fastest recipe in the book, and one of my family's favorites. It goes great with red potatoes and corn on the cob. It's a great summer meal.

2 Tbsp. butter
3 lbs. chicken breast fillets or tenders, cut into strips
   or chunks
1 c. barbecue sauce
1 tsp. Liquid Smoke (optional)
salt and pepper to taste

Melt the butter in your Dutch oven, stir the chicken in, and roast or broast for 10 minutes at 250–300 degrees. Stir in the barbecue sauce, Liquid Smoke (if desired), salt, and pepper. Cook for 2–3 minutes more with the lid off.

Lemon Pepper Chicken

This recipe can be used to cook a roaster or breast fillets; the difference is the time it takes to cook it. I usually do the breast fillets for the time efficiency. This recipe goes equally well with rice or potatoes and a yellow vegetable.

3 lbs. chicken breast fillets or I chicken roaster
juice from 2 lemons
I tsp. lemon zest
I tsp. dried basil or 2 fresh basil leaves
2 tsp. crushed peppercorns
I (14 oz.) can chicken broth
salt to taste

Heat just enough oil to make the bottom of your Dutch oven glossy. Brown the fillets on both sides or, if using a roaster, brown wherever possible. Add the remaining ingredients. If using fillets, roast or broast for 30 minutes at 250–300 degrees. If you are cooking a roaster, bake for 2–3 hours at 225–250 degrees, checking every 30 minutes, basting the meat with a brush. Serve the breasts whole and the roaster quartered, separating the breast pieces, wings, and legs. Note: This works well with game birds too.

Honey Mustard Cutlets

This is a very simple, but very tasty, meal. It definitely goes best with potatoes and a mixed vegetable.

3 lbs. boneless, skinless chicken breasts
¼ c. brown or Dijon mustard
¼ c. honey
juice from 1 orange
2 Tbsp. mayonnaise
¼ c. bread crumbs

Heat just enough oil to make the bottom of your Dutch oven glossy. Then brown the chicken and remove from Dutch oven. Let the meat stand for a few minutes. Mix the mustard, honey, orange juice, and mayonnaise. Coat the chicken breasts thoroughly with the mixture. Lay the breasts in the Dutch oven and sprinkle the bread crumbs over the top. Bake or broast for 20–30 minutes at 300 degrees.

Creamed Spinach Cutlets

This is a great recipe for company. It goes really well with wild or brown rice and a green vegetable. The spinach is very subtle and is a nice complement to the chicken.

2 egg yolks
salt to taste
½ tsp. black pepper
1 c. bread crumbs or crushed Ritz crackers
2 lbs. chicken breast fillets or chicken tenders, cut into strips
1 c. chopped spinach
juice from ½ lemon
1 c. sour cream or plain yogurt
½ c. shredded mozzarella cheese

Start by beating the egg yolks, salt, and pepper in a dish. Spread the bread crumbs or cracker crumbs on a plate. Heat just enough oil to make the bottom of your Dutch oven glossy. Then lightly brown the chicken. In a separate bowl, mix the spinach, lemon juice, sour cream or yogurt, and cheese, and cover the cutlets with this mixture. Bake for 20–30 minutes at 300 degrees.

Mesquite Barbecued Turkey

I have used this recipe for a twist on a Thanksgiving dinner and also for a favorite camping meal. This dish goes well with mashed potatoes and corn.

1 turkey bone-in breast or 1 small turkey
2 (14 oz.) cans chicken broth
1 pkg. McCormick's Mesquite marinade
¼ c. Worcestershire sauce
2 Tbsp. Liquid Smoke
¼ c. barbecue sauce (regular flavor)

Heat just enough oil to make the bottom of your Dutch oven glossy. Quarter the turkey, separating the legs, wings, and breast pieces. Brown the turkey everywhere you can on the outside. Pour the cans of chicken broth into the Dutch oven, and then stir in the remaining ingredients. Place the turkey back in the Dutch oven and roast or broast for 3–4 hours at 225–250 degrees. Check the liquid level every 30 minutes and add water if necessary. This is best if you pull the meat from the bone and allow the meat to soak in the liquid a few minutes before serving.

Chicken Cordon Bleu

Cordon Bleu is a classic. It goes best with a wild or brown rice blend and green vegetables.

    3 lbs. chicken breasts
    ½ lb. grated mozzarella cheese
    ¼ lb. sliced ham
    ¼ c. bleu cheese crumbles
    ¼ c. bread crumbs
    2 egg yolks, whipped
    juice from 1 lemon

Start by pounding out the chicken breasts between 2 sheets of plastic wrap or waxed paper. In a bowl, mix the mozzarella, ham, and bleu cheese. Spread the mixture onto one side of the chicken breast. Fold the chicken over and pin it closed with a toothpick. Dip the chicken in the egg yolks and roll in the bread crumbs. Heat just enough oil to make the bottom of your Dutch oven glossy. Lightly brown the chicken on both sides. Squeeze the lemon juice on top of the chicken. Bake for 30 minutes at 300 degrees. Serve with Spinach & Mushroom Sauce.

Spinach & Mushroom Sauce

    4 Tbsp. butter
    ½ c. chopped mushrooms
    1 c. chopped spinach
    3 Tbsp. honey
    1 c. heavy cream
    2 egg yolks, whipped

In your Dutch oven, melt the butter and brown the mushrooms and spinach. Slowly stir in the honey and the cream. Finish by stirring in the egg yolks until the sauce has thickened to where you would like it. Drizzle the sauce liberally over your Cordon Bleu fillets.

Pork Recipes

With the exception of the recipes where I specify to use a pork loin roll, any pork will do in the following recipes. I use a lot of cushion pork in my own cooking. Cushion pork is the loin ends that are somewhat triangular in shape. You can pick up cushion pork at your local meat cutters for a fantastic price, and as a double benefit, it is very low in fat.

Black Forest Loin Roast
Aussie-Style Pulled Pork
Peppercorn & Garlic Roast
Hawaiian-Style Pork Roast
Southern-Style Pulled Pork
Apple Barbecued Spare Ribs
Summer Chipotle Loin Roast

Black Forest Loin Roast

This is a German pork recipe and, although it's traditionally served with a pasta, I prefer it with rice or potatoes and a green vegetable.

½ c. chopped dried apricots
½ c. chopped prunes
4 fresh mint leaves, finely chopped
I c. sparkling apple cider
I (2–3 lb.) pork loin roll
I (14 oz.) can chicken broth
I c. heavy cream

Begin by chopping the apricots, prunes, and mint. Place it in a baggy with the sparkling cider and let it sit for at least an hour. Run a thin knife through the center of the roast and twist it around to form a pocket. Fill the pocket with the fruit mix. Heat just enough oil to make the bottom of your Dutch oven glossy. Brown all sides of the roast then remove and let the roast stand for 15 minutes. Place back in the Dutch oven and broast at 300 degrees for thirty minutes. Use the broth just to keep a little liquid in the bottom of the Dutch oven. After 30 minutes, pour the cream over the roast and cook 5 minutes longer. To serve, slice the roast into ¾-inch slices and drizzle the cream mixture on the top.

Aussie-Style Pulled Pork

Pulled pork has recently made a comeback because of its great taste and versatility. It can be served as a stand-alone meal or in a sandwich. It is best served with mashed potatoes and corn on the cob.

1 (2–3) lb. pork roast, any style
1 large sweet onion, chopped
2 c. apple juice
2 tsp. coarse black pepper
2 Tbsp. mustard
2 Tbsp. Liquid Smoke, hickory flavor
1 c. barbecue sauce, regular flavor

Heat just enough oil to make the bottom of your Dutch oven glossy. Brown the roast on all sides, browning the onion at the same time. Add the apple juice, pepper, mustard, and Liquid Smoke. Broast at 300 degrees for 2–3 hours or until the meat can be pulled easily. Add the barbecue sauce and then pull the meat apart with forks before serving.

Peppercorn & Garlic Roast

This is a great recipe and goes well with wild rice and asparagus.

1 (2–3 lb.) pork loin roll
6 garlic cloves, sliced
2 c. white grape juice
1 sprig fresh rosemary
2 Tbsp. crushed black peppercorns

Begin by inserting a thin-bladed knife randomly into the roast and inserting garlic slices into the slits. Brown the roast thoroughly on all sides. Remove the roast and let it stand for 15 minutes. While the Dutch oven is hot, add the grape juice and the rosemary sprig. Rub the peppercorns into the roast and return the roast to the Dutch oven. Broast for 30–40 minutes, adding water as necessary. Slice the roast into 1-inch thick slices.

Hawaiian-Style Pork Roast

This is the luau-style pork done in a smaller portion. It is best served with white rice, chow mein noodles, and summer vegetables.

I (2–3 lb.) pork shoulder or sirloin roast
I large sweet onion
I (20 oz.) can crushed pineapple or 2 c. fresh pineapple
3 garlic cloves, crushed
4 Tbsp. brown sugar
4 Tbsp. Liquid Smoke, hickory flavor
¼ c. soy sauce
I (14 oz.) can chicken broth

Heat just enough oil to make the bottom of your Dutch oven glossy. Brown the roast on all sides. Add the remaining ingredients and roast or broast for 2–5 hours at 300 degrees. You should be able to pull the meat apart easily before serving. Add liquid as needed.

Southern-Style Pulled Pork

This recipe is similar to the Aussie-Style, but it's sticky sweet in comparison. This is the pulled pork most people have tried. It goes well with just about everything.

I (2–3 lb.) pork roast, any type
I medium sweet onion, chopped
¼ c. brown sugar
I (14 oz.) can chicken broth
2 Tbsp. molasses
2 c. barbecue sauce

Heat just enough oil to make the bottom of your Dutch oven glossy. Brown the roast on all sides, browning the onion at the same time. Add the sugar, broth, and molasses. Broast for 3–5 hours or until the meat pulls apart easily. Check often and add liquid as necessary. Stir in the barbecue sauce. Simmer for 10 minutes. Pull the meat apart with forks before serving.

Apple Barbecued Ribs

I love spare ribs and these are the best. Being a Southern dish, this recipe goes best with corn on the cob and corn bread.

1 slab of spare ribs
1 c. apple juice
4 Tbsp. Liquid Smoke, hickory flavored
1 (14 oz.) can chicken broth
1 c. barbecue sauce

Heat just enough oil to make the bottom of your Dutch oven glossy. Brown the convex side of the ribs. Split the ribs if necessary to fit in the Dutch oven, placing concave side down. Pour in the apple juice and Liquid Smoke. Broast for 1–2 hours at 300 degrees, checking often and adding the chicken broth as needed to keep the liquid level about a quarter of the way up the meat. Add more broth if the sauce looks too thick. When the meat can easily be pulled apart, pour in the barbecue sauce and broast for 10 more minutes.

Summer Chipotle Loin Roast

This is one of my favorite pork recipes. If you have ever been to one of my demos, this is more than likely what you tried. This is great served with yellow squash, red peppers, and potatoes, and I often cook them all in the same Dutch oven.

1 (2–3 lb.) pork loin roast
1 pkg. McCormick's Chipotle marinade
1 (14 oz.) can chicken broth
salt to taste
vegetables of your choice

Heat just enough oil to make the bottom of your Dutch oven glossy. Brown the roast on all sides, then remove and let stand for 15 minutes. Rub the marinade all over the roast; return to the Dutch oven along with half the broth. Roast or broast for 15 minutes at 300 degrees, then add the remaining broth and any vegetables you want. Cook an additional 15 minutes.

Seafood Recipes

Seafood overall is my favorite food to eat. Here is a selection of some of my favorite recipes. If you can buy fresh seafood, do so. When seafood is frozen and thawed, some of the delicate proteins and fats will break down, causing a fishy flavor that none of us like. Be careful not to overlook seafood. Just like thawing, over-cooking will cause it to break down and taste bad. The best indicator for fish is the color change. When it is done cooking, the meat will be uniform in color.

Shrimp Scampi
Sweet Dill Salmon
Egg-Battered Fillets
Beach-Grilled Fillets
Honey Mustard Fillets
Tomato & Basil Fillets
English Battered Halibut
Parmesan Crusted Fillets
Corn-Breaded Catfish Fillets

Shrimp Scampi

Shrimp Scampi is definitely one of my family's favorite meals. It goes best with asparagus and jasmine rice.

4 Tbsp. butter
4 cloves garlic, crushed
3 lbs. fresh medium shrimp, peeled and de-veined
juice from 2 lemons
2 tsp. coarse black pepper
½ c. sour cream
¼ lb. grated mozzarella cheese

Begin by melting the butter in the bottom of the Dutch oven. Lightly toast the garlic. Then add the shrimp, lemon juice, and pepper. Cover the Dutch oven and roast at low heat, about 200 degrees, for 5 minutes. Add the sour cream and cheese, and then roast for 5 minutes more.

Tip: For a lower-fat recipe, you can replace the sour cream with plain yogurt and replace the butter with ½ c. white grape juice.

Sweet Dill Salmon

This is my all-time favorite way to prepare salmon. Serve this with rice or potatoes and a green vegetable.

2 (1 lb.) skinned salmon fillets
juice from 1 lemon
3 tsp. dill weed
2 Tbsp. brown sugar
2 tsp. Liquid Smoke, hickory flavor
2 Tbsp. butter
1 c. white grape juice
salt to taste

Start by peeling the skin off the salmon and removing the lateral line. In a bowl, combine the lemon, dill, sugar, and Liquid Smoke. Rub this mixture into the salmon fillets. In your Dutch oven, melt the butter and sear the salmon. Pour the white grape juice over the top, and broast at 300 degrees for 30 minutes.

Egg-Battered Fillets

This is a great recipe for those looking for a healthy battered fish. It goes well with flavored rice and a green vegetable.

3 egg yolks, whipped
¼ c. bread crumbs
flour as needed
2 lbs. white fish fillets
juice from 1 lemon

Mix egg yolks and bread crumbs. Add flour until a thick pancake-like batter forms. Roll the fillets in the batter and place in your Dutch oven. Bake at 300 degrees for 30–40 minutes or until the batter is golden brown. Squeeze the lemon on the fillets and let stand for 2–3 minutes before serving.

Beach-Grilled Fillets

This recipe is great for any sort of boneless white fish fillets. This is meant to be eaten Tex-Mex style with fried tortillas and fresh mango salsa.

2 Tbsp. butter

3 lbs. white fish fillets (bass, perch, catfish, mahi-mahi, etc.)

4 tsp. ground New Mexico chile powder (not chili powder)

juice from 2 limes

1 pinch lime zest

salt to taste

1 roma tomato, diced

Melt the butter in the bottom of your Dutch oven. Lightly sear the fillets and add the remaining ingredients except tomato. Broast for 15–20 minutes. Add the tomato and let it sit for 5 minutes before serving.

Honey Mustard Fillets

This recipe works best with catfish but any white fish fillets will do.
Serve with white rice and a green vegetable.

¼ c. brown mustard
¼ c. honey
4 Tbsp. mayonnaise
2 lbs. catfish fillets
½ c. bread crumbs

Begin by mixing the mustard, honey, and mayonnaise together. Spread this mixture on the fillets. Set the fillets in your Dutch oven and sprinkle with the bread crumbs. Broast for 20 minutes at 350 degrees.

Tomato & Basil Fillets

This is a Mediterranean dish that works best with sea bass, but you can also use most firm white fish fillets. I like to serve this dish with pasta and a clam sauce and a pepper medley.

6 Tbsp. sun-dried tomato pesto
2 lbs. sea bass fillets
½ c. white grape juice
4 garlic cloves, crushed

Begin by brushing the pesto onto the fillets and placing them into your Dutch oven. Slowly pour the grape juice into the Dutch oven and add the garlic. Broast for 20–30 minutes at 300 degrees.

English-Battered Halibut

I have tried battered halibut all over the country. The best I have tried so far is in Juneau, Alaska. Anyone familiar with Juneau knows the two establishments I am talking about. Not only is their halibut fresh, but the batter is excellent. I have spent eight years trying to come close and have finally done so. I hope you enjoy.

12 oz. apple juice
1 pinch salt
flour
enough canola oil to fill the Dutch oven 1/4 full
3 lbs. Halibut, cut into square chunks

Combine apple juice, salt, and enough flour to reach the consistency of pancake batter. If you dip a spoon in, it should coat it but not clump. Heat up the oil to about 350 degrees. Carefully drop the battered halibut into the oil. Fry for about 5 minutes or until the batter is golden. Turn the fish over and fry the other side for about 5 minutes as well. Let the halibut relax on a paper towel for several minutes before serving.

Parmesan-Crusted Fillets

I tried this recipe in Minnesota and fell in love with it. I think it tastes best with walleye or perch fillets, though it works well with bass or tilapia as well. Serve with wild rice and squash.

1 egg, whipped
¼ c. mayonnaise (for less fat, use plain yogurt)
½ c. crushed Ritz crackers
¼ c. grated parmesan cheese (not powdered)
2 lbs. walleye fillets
juice of 1 lemon

Begin by mixing the egg and mayonnaise and brushing it on to the fillets. Place the fillets in the Dutch oven. Mix the crackers and cheese and sprinkle over the fillets. Squeeze the lemon onto the fillets and broast for 30 minutes.

Corn-Breaded Catfish Fillets

This is a Southern favorite, best served with hush puppies and greens.

2 eggs, whipped
I c. warm water
I c. buttermilk
I c. crumbled corn bread or cornmeal
3 tsp. baking powder
flour as needed
I Tbsp. vinegar
enough canola oil to fill the Dutch oven 1/4 full
2 lbs. catfish fillets
salt to taste

To begin, heat a small amount of oil in your Dutch oven to 350 degrees. Mix the eggs, water, buttermilk, cornmeal or corn bread, and baking powder. Add the flour until the batter reaches the consistency of thick pancake batter. Stir in the vinegar slowly. Dip the catfish fillets in the batter and set them in the oil. Cover and cook for 5 minutes or until they are golden brown on the bottom. Turn them over and cook another 5 minutes. Let the fillets stand on a paper towel for 2–3 minutes before serving.

Game Recipes

Cooking wild game is a specialty of mine. There is no tool better than a Dutch oven to cook wild game. I have included recipes for a mixed bag of game. As far as health is concerned, there isn't a healthier meat on earth. Wild meat is extremely low in fat and cholesterol. Because of this, care must be taken not to overcook it.

**Venison Dijon
Cola Venison Tips
Southern-Fried Bass
Chuckwagon Steaks
Emerald City Halibut
Southern-Style Dove
Wild Mountain Goose
Rocky Mountain Trout
Mesquite Grouse Fillets
Northern Lights Salmon
Mesquite Venison Loin Strips
Bacon-Wrapped Pheasant Cuts
Pineapple-Glazed Venison Roast**

Venison Dijon

This recipe is easy to make and goes wonderfully with fried potatoes and corn on the cob.

½ lb. bacon
1 lb. venison steaks
6 Tbsp. Dijon mustard
3 Tbsp. honey
2 Tbsp. mayonnaise
1 Tbsp. vinegar

Wrap bacon around circumference of steaks. Mix the mustard, honey, mayonnaise, and vinegar in a bowl. Heat just enough oil to make the bottom of your Dutch oven glossy. Sear both sides of the steak. Then brush on the mustard glaze. Broast for 15–20 minutes, turning twice, continually basting with the glaze. Serve immediately.

Cola Venison Tips

I am not even sure where the idea for this recipe came from. I have been cooking this recipe for a few years, tweaking it until I felt I had it just right. One thing is for sure: it is a crowd favorite! Serve this over rice. I also like to serve it with green vegetables, such as fresh green beans with balsamic vinegar.

I lb. venison steaks
I medium sharp onion, chopped
salt to taste
I can Coca-Cola
I c. water
3 Tbsp. vinegar
I tsp. fresh basil
2 cubes beef bouillon
¼ c. Worcestershire sauce
3 Tbsp. Liquid Smoke, mesquite flavor
2 cloves garlic, minced
¼ c. mushrooms, chopped
cornstarch to thicken

In a Dutch oven, brown the steaks in a little oil. Add the onions and salt. Stir-fry until the onions are clear. Add the Coca-Cola, water, vinegar, basil, bouillon, Worcestershire sauce, Liquid Smoke, and garlic. Roast for 1 to 1½ hours at 300 degrees or until the meat is tender. Add the mushrooms and thicken with the starch.

Southern-Fried Bass

This recipe is a Southern favorite best served with hush puppies and greens. This works best with bass, but any white fish will do.

2 lbs. bass fillets
I c. flour
½ c. bread crumbs
¼ c. cornmeal
2 tsp. baking powder
I tsp. salt
½ tsp. cayenne pepper

In a large bowl, mix all the ingredients except the fish. Add water until the batter reaches the consistency of pancake batter. Heat up a small amount of oil in your Dutch oven to about 350 degrees. Gently set the fillets in the oil and cook for 5 minutes or until the batter is golden brown in color. Turn the fillets over and cook until the fillets are the same color as the other side. Remove from the oil and let the fillets stand for 2–3 minutes before serving.

Chuckwagon Steaks

This recipe works wonderfully for camping because it's so easy. It goes well with Dutch oven potatoes or beans. I usually reserve this recipe for camp dinners, but it is great any time you want an outdoor meal.

1 lb. venison steaks
1 lb. bacon
1 large sweet onion, chopped
1 drop hot sauce per steak, like Tapatio or Tabasco
salt to taste
black pepper to taste

Sear the steaks on both sides in a little oil in your Dutch oven. Place the bacon, onion, and hot sauce on top of the steaks. Cover and broast for 10–15 minutes at 350 degrees. Add salt and pepper. Serve immediately.

Emerald City Halibut

I call this one the Emerald City because the Seattle area is the largest provider of halibut, other than Alaska, and all the ingredients in this recipe are green. I like to serve this with brown rice, a summer squash, and a bell pepper medley for the balance of taste and flavor it creates.

2 Tbsp. chopped parsley
2 Tbsp. chopped basil
2 tsp. dill weed
2 Tbsp. butter
2–3 lbs. halibut fillets
I Tbsp. brown sugar
¼ c. white grape juice
¼ c. cream
juice from I lime

Begin by chopping the parsley and basil. Mix together with the dill and set aside. Melt the butter in the bottom of your Dutch oven. Add the fillets and lightly brown them on both sides. Add the herbs and the brown sugar. Slowly stir in the white grape juice. Bake for 30 minutes at 300 degrees. Stir the cream in slowly and let it stand for 5 minutes. Squeeze the lime over the top.

Southern-Style Dove

I learned this recipe from a friend who lives for dove hunting. This is his favorite way to prepare dove. This recipe goes equally well with rice or potatoes and is matched perfect with corn on the cob.

10–15 dove breast fillets, removed from the bone
½ c. buttermilk
3 egg yolks, whipped
1 tsp. salt
1 c. bread crumbs
1 tsp. cayenne pepper

Begin by placing the dove breasts and the buttermilk in a plastic bag. Place in the fridge or a cooler for at least an hour. Whip the eggs and salt in a bowl. Mix the bread crumbs and cayenne pepper on a plate. Dip the dove meat in the egg mixture and roll in the crumbs. Set the meat in your Dutch oven with a small amount of oil, heated up to 350 degrees. Broast for 5 minutes and turn over. Broast for another 10 minutes.

Wild Mountain Goose

This is a recipe I tried out for a cooking demo and it turned out awesome. I have had a lot of people tell me they no longer feel guilty hunting waterfowl because they love to eat them now.

I goose, quartered
½ c. flour
I sweet onion, sliced
2 c. cranberry juice
I (14 oz.) can chicken broth
I Tbsp. Liquid Smoke, hickory flavored
I c. chopped mushrooms
½ c. chopped celery tops
4 cloves garlic
salt to taste
½ c. cream

Begin by rinsing off the goose quarters. While they are damp, sprinkle the flour on the meat. In your Dutch oven, heat up a small amount of oil and caramelize the onion. Brown the goose on as many sides as possible. Add the cranberry juice, broth, and Liquid Smoke. Broast for 2–3 hours at 250 degrees. Add the mushrooms, celery, garlic, and salt. Broast for another 10 minutes. Add the cream and simmer 5 minutes. Serve the meat pulled.

Rocky Mountain Trout

This recipe is a camping favorite. It's best with fresh trout. This recipe goes well with any potato-and-vegetable combination.

3 Tbsp. butter
2 tsp. garlic salt
4–8 trout fillets, skinned and pin bones removed
juice from 1 lemon
½ c. crushed Ritz crackers

Begin by melting the butter in the Dutch oven and mixing in the garlic salt. Lightly sear the trout on both sides. Squeeze the lemon on the fish and sprinkle the Ritz crackers over the top of the fillets. Bake at 300 degrees for 15 minutes.

Mesquite Grouse Fillets

I love to eat grouse, and this is my favorite way to prepare it. The mesquite compliments the grouse very well. I like to serve it with potatoes and a green vegetable.

4 grouse breasts, filleted off the bone
1 pkg. McCormick's mesquite marinade
3 cloves garlic, sliced
2 Tbsp. butter

Heat just enough oil to make the bottom of your Dutch oven glossy. Sear the grouse fillets well on both sides. Add the marinade mix liberally on top of the meat. Roast for 10 minutes at 300 degrees. Remove the grouse and set aside. Place the garlic and butter in your Dutch oven. Split the grouse breast in half, thickness-wise, or cut into strips. Place back in the Dutch oven. Stir-fry for 30–45 seconds and remove heat. Let stand for 2–3 minutes before serving.

Northern Lights
Salmon

This is a recipe I tried once on a whim, and it turned out to be something I really enjoy. It goes well with asparagus and rice.

2 Tbsp. butter
2–3 lbs. salmon fillets, skinned and pin bones removed
½ c. blueberries, crushed
½ c. raspberries, crushed
1 lemon, sliced
½ tsp. coarse black pepper
salt to taste

Begin by melting the butter in the bottom of your Dutch oven. Lightly sear both sides of the salmon. In a separate bowl, mix the blueberries, raspberries, and the lemon slices. Slowly add it into the Dutch oven. Add the pepper to the top of the fillets. Cover and bake for 20 minutes at 350 degrees. Add the salt and serve.

Mesquite Venison Loin Strips

This recipe is probably one of my all-time favorite venison recipes. It has a little spice to it, but it's not overwhelming. This meal is suited best as a Tex-Mex-style dish served with beans, rice, and tortillas.

> **1 lb. venison steaks**
> **4 cloves garlic, sliced, or 4 tsp. minced garlic**
> **1 pkg. dry McCormick's mesquite marinade mix**
> **¼ stick butter**
> **¼ c. Worcestershire sauce**

Heat just enough oil to make the bottom of your Dutch oven glossy. Continue to heat until it begins to smoke. Brown the steaks. Mix the garlic and dry marinade mix and apply liberally to steaks after they have been turned over. When meat has sweated twice, remove from Dutch oven. Add butter and Worcestershire sauce to the hot oven and remove from heat. Cut steaks lengthwise in strips and add back to sauce. Stir well before serving.

Bacon-Wrapped Pheasant

It may not be the healthiest way to cook pheasant, but bacon sure makes it taste good. I like this best with white rice and asparagus.

½ lb. thick-sliced bacon
2 cloves garlic, minced
2–3 pheasant breasts, filleted off the bone
½ c. apple juice
1 slice Swiss cheese for each breast fillet
¼ c. cream
salt to taste

Begin by laying the strips of bacon on a sheet of plastic wrap next to one another. Sprinkle with garlic and place the breast fillets on top. Roll the plastic up so the bacon wraps all the way around the breast. Remove the plastic wrap; the bacon will stay on. Heat just enough oil to make the bottom of your Dutch oven glossy. Set the fillets in with the end of the bacon down so it doesn't come unwrapped. Sear for 2–3 minutes on each side. Pour the apple juice in the Dutch oven and bake at 350 degrees for 20 minutes. Set the Swiss cheese on the fillets, add the cream, and broil for 5 minutes.

Pineapple-Glazed Venison Roast

This is a great-tasting recipe of my own creation. It is best served with Dutch oven potatoes and yellow vegetables.

1 center-cut venison roast, such as a loin or center round
½ c. apple cider
¼ c. crushed pineapple
2 Tbsp. crushed black pepper
2 Tbsp. molasses
1 tsp. crushed cloves
2 Tbsp. brown sugar
juice from 1 lemon

Heat just enough oil to make the bottom of your Dutch oven glossy. Brown the roast on all sides. Create rub by combining all remaining ingredients and blending into a puree. Apply rub to the roast liberally and broast for a little over 1 hour at 350 degrees, adding liquid in small amounts as necessary. Slice the roast cross-grain and let it relax in the sauce for 15–20 minutes before serving.

Soups and Stews

Dutch Ovens work very well for soups and stews, to the point where I won't cook a soup outside of a Dutch oven. These recipes are some of my favorites.

Best Beef Stew
Potato Chowder
Bacon Bean Soup
French Onion Soup
Boston Clam Chowder
Cheddar Broccoli Soup
Ham and Navy Bean Soup
Homestyle Chicken Noodle
Chicken and Wild Rice Soup
Chicken Cream Tomato Soup

Best Beef Stew

This recipe is a no-holds-barred, all-included beef stew. There are a million recipes out there, but this is my favorite.

¼ c. canola oil
¼ c. flour
1 large sweet onion, chopped
2–3 lbs. beef steak, cubed
½ lb. breakfast sausage links
3 cloves garlic, sliced
2 bay leaves
6–8 red potatoes, washed and cubed
½ c. sliced carrots
½ c. sliced celery
3 (14 oz.) cans beef broth, divided
4 Tbsp. Worcestershire sauce
Salt and pepper to taste

Begin by mixing the oil and the flour in the Dutch oven and heating to 300 degrees, stirring often until it is a milk chocolate color. Slowly stir in the onion, beef, and sausage. Brown. Add all the remaining ingredients, except 1 can of broth. Roast for 30–45 minutes at 350 degrees or until the meat is tender. Check often, adding broth as necessary. Thicken to desired consistency with starch.

Potato Chowder

This is a German recipe, and it is sometimes called Ham Chowder. It is extremely easy to make.

¼ stick butter
2 tsp. black pepper
2 cloves garlic, minced
6 c. diced potatoes
2 c. cubed ham
3 (14 oz.) cans chicken broth
½ c. chopped celery
½ c. chopped carrots
starch to thicken
4 c. heavy cream

Begin by heating up your Dutch oven and adding in the butter, pepper, garlic, and potatoes. Stir in the ham and chicken broth. Roast at 300 degrees for 20–30 minutes or until the potatoes are tender. Add the celery and carrots. Roast for 10–15 minutes. Thicken with the starch. Slowly stir in the cream.

Bacon Bean Soup

This is a camping classic, guaranteed to keep you warm and full on a cold night.

- 1 lb. bacon, chopped
- 1 small sweet onion, chopped
- 3 (14 oz.) cans pinto beans
- 2 Tbsp. butter
- ¼ c. brown sugar or honey
- 1 bay leaf
- 1 (14 oz.) can chicken broth
- 1 pinch nutmeg

Begin by frying the bacon and the onion together in your Dutch oven. Cook until browned. Add the remaining ingredients. Roast at 350 degrees for 45 minutes. To thicken the soup, mash some of the beans. The more you mash, the thicker it becomes.

French Onion Soup

Anyone who has had a French dip sandwich has tried a version of French Onion Soup with the au jous. The soup evolved as a way to stretch out meals further. Now it has become a classic soup.

1 large sweet onion, chopped
¼ stick butter
8 oz. leftover steak, chopped small
5 Tbsp. flour
4 (14 oz.) cans beef broth
2 bay leaves
2 c. croutons
¼ lb. shredded mozzarella

Begin by caramelizing the onion in the butter until the onion is clear. Add the steak and flour. Stir-fry until the steak is well browned. Add the broth and bay leaves. Roast for 20–30 minutes at 300 degrees. Place the croutons on top and sprinkle with cheese. Do not stir! Bake or broil the soup for another 10 minutes. Serve. If it is done right, the cheese and croutons will form a layer on the top of the soup.

Boston Clam Chowder

I love clam chowder. I spent some time in New England and I fell in love with this variation of clam chowder.

½ stick butter
2 small cans baby clams, cut into strips
4 cloves garlic, minced
1 tsp. celery seed
4 c. diced red potatoes
2 (14 oz.) cans chicken broth
1 Roma tomato, diced
1 c. chopped spinach
½ c. celery
starch to thicken
4 c. cream

Begin by melting the butter and adding the clams, garlic, and celery seed. Stir for 2–3 minutes. Add the potatoes and chicken broth. Roast at 300 degrees for 20–30 minutes or until the potatoes are tender. Add the tomatoes, spinach, and celery. Roast for 10 minutes. Thicken with the starch until it reaches the desired consistency. Slowly stir in the cream.

Cheddar Broccoli Soup

This is one of my favorite soup recipes. It is also extremely easy to prepare.

¼ stick butter
4 cloves garlic, crushed
6–8 c. broccoli florets, cut into bite-sized pieces
2 (14 oz.) cans vegetable broth
starch to thicken
2 c. heavy cream
1/3 lb. cheddar cheese, grated

Begin by melting the butter and lightly stir-frying the garlic. Add the broccoli and the vegetable broth. Roast for 20 minutes or until the broccoli is tender. Thicken the soup with the starch until it reaches the desired consistency. Slowly stir in the cream and cheese. Cook until cheese has melted.

Ham and Navy Bean Soup

This is a recipe my dad used to make for us a lot. It still is one of my favorite soups, and it's so easy to make.

1 large sweet onion, chopped
2 Tbsp. butter
2 c. cubed ham
3 (14 oz.) cans drained navy or great northern beans
2 bay leaves
2 (14 oz.) cans chicken broth
salt to taste

Begin by caramelizing the onion in the butter. Add the ham and lightly brown it. Add the remaining ingredients. Roast for at least 1 hour at 300 degrees, checking often and adding water as necessary. When you are done, either add water or mash the beans to gain your desired thickness.

# Homestyle Chicken Noodle

This is a slight twist on an American classic. It still has the comfort-food quality but now with a little kick. For this recipe I use a blonde roux. A blonde roux is a golden color.

4 Tbsp. flour
4 Tbsp. canola oil
1 medium onion, chopped
½ c. chopped celery
½ c. sliced carrots
2 lbs. boneless skinless chicken breasts, chopped
3 (14 oz.) cans chicken broth
2 bay leaves
2 tsp. New Mexico chile powder (mild)

Noodles:
2 egg yolks, whipped
1 c. warm water, divided
1 pinch salt
½ tsp. brown sugar
1 c. bread flour

Begin by making a blonde roux. To do this, whisk the flour and oil together in your Dutch oven at 300 degrees for 5–10 minutes or until the mixture is a golden color. Add the onion, celery, and carrots, stirring slowly. Add the chicken. Keep the mixture cooking until the chicken is browned. Add the broth, bay leaves, and chile powder. Roast for 30 minutes at 350 degrees. To make the noodles, whip the egg yolks and add half of the warm water. Add the salt and brown sugar. Slowly stir in the flour and knead until a dough forms. Roll out and cut thinly into strips. Drop the strips in 5 minutes before you want to serve the soup.

Chicken & Wild Rice Soup

This is a soup I ate a lot in Minnesota, the land of wild rice. It's a great way to eat this wild grain.

2 Tbsp. vegetable oil
2 Tbsp. flour
I medium onion, chopped
I lb. chicken
½ c. diced ham
I c. wild rice, uncooked
½ c. chopped celery
½ c. chopped carrots
3 (14 oz.) cans chicken broth
I c. mushrooms
I tsp. rosemary
I tsp. parsley
salt and pepper to taste

Begin by creating a blonde roux by mixing the oil and flour and heating it until it becomes golden in color. Add the onion, chicken, ham, and rice. Cook until the meat is browned. Add the remaining ingredients and roast for 30–45 minutes at 300 degrees or until the rice is tender.

Chicken Cream Tomato Soup

This recipe was an experiment gone right. It is a great soup to eat with a sandwich.

1 (8 oz.) pkg. cream cheese
4 Tbsp. butter
1 small sharp onion, chopped
2–3 lbs. boneless skinless chicken breasts, chopped
2 (14 oz.) cans chicken broth
2 bay leaves
4 large tomatoes, chopped
2 Tbsp. chopped fresh basil
juice from 1 lemon
½ c. cream
starch to thicken, if needed

Allow the cream cheese to come to room temperature or microwave for 30 seconds. Set aside. Melt the butter in the Dutch oven. Add the onion; brown. Add the chopped chicken and stir until lightly browned. Add the remaining ingredients, except the cream cheese, cream, and starch. Roast for 30–45 minutes at 350 degrees. In a separate bowl, whip the cream cheese and cream. Slowly add this mixture to the soup, stirring until it is dissolved.

Chilis

There is a huge distinction between the two types of chilis. It's clearly defined by the border. Mexican chiles (not chilis) are simply a pulled meat that has been slow-cooked in a chile pepper sauce. The thickness and consistency in a chile is created using masa or corn flour. You can use crushed tortilla chips just as well as masa. American chilis are a southwestern spin-off created by camp cooks on cattle drives in the late 1800s. Most people are more familiar with the American chilis (meat, beans, tomatoes, and spice). I have included several of my favorite chili recipes of both types.

Barbacoa
Masa Chile
Green Chile
Tres Carnes
Trailboss Chili
Triple Three Chili
Beaver Mountain Chili

Barbacoa

This is the traditional Mexican party dish that is served at weddings and birthdays. The traditional recipe is made from goat meat, but beef or pork roast makes a good substitute. Some of the ingredients have to be purchased in a Mexican food store.

- 1 large beef or pork roast
- 1 large sweet onion, chopped
- 4 cloves garlic, minced
- 4 tsp. cumin
- 4 Tbsp. powdered anatole seed
- 2 Tbsp. Mexican oregano
- 2 Tbsp. New Mexico chiles, powdered
- 4 dried whole arbol chiles
- juice from 3 limes
- 1 Tbsp. crushed black pepper
- 4 Tbsp. vinegar
- ¼ c. fresh cilantro, chopped
- 2 (8 oz.) cans tomato sauce

Combine all the ingredients in your Dutch oven; add enough water to cover one-third of the roast. Do not add any more unless it needs it. Roast or broast for 3–5 hours at 300 degrees or until the meat can be pulled apart easily with a fork. Pull the meat and let it relax in the sauce for 5–10 minutes before serving.

Masa Chile

This is a true Mexican chile made thick by adding corn tortilla chips. It can be made with any type of meat. This is the traditional red chile. Serve with tortillas, beans, and rice.

2–3 lbs. meat (any type)
1 large sweet onion, chopped
5 Tbsp. vegetable oil
3 large tomatoes, diced
3 limes, squeezed
2 cloves garlic, minced
1 Tbsp. New Mexico chile powder
1 jalapeño, seeded and veined
3 tsp. cumin
5 Tbsp. cider vinegar
1 (7 oz.) can Chipotle peppers
1 (14 oz.) can chicken broth
2 c. crushed corn tortilla chips

Begin by chopping up the meat and onion. Brown in the oil until the onion is clear. Add the remaining ingredients except the chips. Roast for 2–3 hours at 300 degrees, adding water as needed. Add the chips and stir well. Cook 10–15 minutes more. Garnish with fresh cilantro.

Green Chile

This is the other side of the chile. While most of us are familiar with the red style, the green is more popular in some regions of Mexico where the tomatillo grows better. Serve with tortillas, beans, and rice.

2–3 lbs. chicken or pork
1 large sweet onion, chopped
juice of 3 limes
2 cloves garlic, minced
4 jalapenos, veined and seeded
1 Anaheim pepper, veined and seeded
2 tsp. cumin
2 tsp. Mexican oregano
1 (14 oz.) can chicken broth
salt to taste
2 lbs. whole tomatillos, peeled

Heat just enough oil to make the bottom of your Dutch oven glossy. Brown the meat on all sides while carmelizing the onions at the same time. Place the rest of the ingredients (except the tomatillos) in the Dutch oven and roast or broast for 2–3 hours at 350 degrees, checking regularly and adding liquid as needed. When the meat is tender, pull it apart with forks. Mash the tomatillos and mix them into the chile.

Tres Carnes

Tres Carnes (Three Meats) is so named because there are three different types of meat in it. This is a great chile to make for company. Because of its mild, intricate flavor, it is sure to please. Serve it Tex-Mex style with tortillas, beans, and rice.

1 lb. beef chuck, cubed
1 lb. pork shoulder, cubed
1 lb. chorizo or country-style pork sausage
1 large sweet onion, chopped
2 roasted jalapeño peppers
1 roasted Anaheim pepper
2 large tomatoes, diced
2 bay leaves
3 Tbsp. New Mexico chile powder (mild)
2 c. apple juice
2 tsp. cumin
juice from 2 limes
4 Tbsp. brown sugar
2 Tbsp. cocoa
4 chicken bouillon cubes
5 Tbsp. vinegar
¼ c. chopped cilantro
1 c. crushed tortilla chips

Begin by browning the meats, onion, and peppers in your Dutch oven. Add all remaining ingredients and roast or broast for 3–5 hours at 300 degrees. Check often, adding water as necessary. After each hour, mash the meat. When it is all mashed well, serve garnished with fresh cilantro and onions.

Tip:
Roast the peppers over high heat until the skin blackens. Remove the skin and use the soft, flavorful pepper underneath.

Trailboss Chili

This is the American chili I cook the most. It is extremely easy and tastes great.

I lb. cubed beef steak
I lb. breakfast sausage, sliced
I (28 oz.) can crushed tomatoes
I medium sweet onion
I (14 oz.) can pinto beans, drained
2 (14 oz.) cans black beans, drained
¼ c. honey or brown sugar
4 Tbsp. hot sauce
2 Tbsp. butter
5 Tbsp. vinegar

Begin by browning the meat and onions in your Dutch oven. Add the remaining ingredients and roast for 1 hour at 300 degrees or until the meat is tender. Before serving, mash the chili until it reaches the desired thickness.

Triple Three Chili

This is one of my favorite American chilis—three meats, three beans, three peppers. This recipe is not for beginners!

1 lb. cubed beef (round or sirloin)
1 lb. cubed pork
1 lb. breakfast sausage, sliced
1 large sweet onion, chopped
1 (14 oz.) can pinto beans, drained
1 (14 oz.) can black beans, drained
1 (14 oz.) can red beans, drained
4 cloves garlic, minced
1 (10.5 oz.) can crushed tomatoes
2 jalapeño peppers, chopped, veined, and seeded
2 habanero peppers, chopped, veined, and seeded
2 Anaheim peppers, chopped, veined, and seeded
2 Tbsp. New Mexico chile powder
1 (14 oz.) can beef broth
1 (14 oz.) can chicken broth
2 bay leaves
1 tsp. cumin
2 Tbsp. molasses
salt to taste

Begin by browning the meat and onion. Add the remaining ingredients and roast at least 3 hours at 300 degrees. Check and stir often, adding liquid as necessary. When the chili is done, use a potato masher to mash it until it reaches the desired thickness. The more you mash it, the thicker it will be. Garnish with fresh onions, tomatoes, cilantro, and cheese.

Beaver Mountain Chili

This is a recipe that started as a deer hunting tradition. The recipe comes from my dad. He cooked this every year on the night before the opener.

1–2 lbs. extra-lean ground beef
1–2 large sweet onions
2 (28 oz.) cans crushed tomatoes
1 red bell pepper, chopped
1 green bell pepper, chopped
1 jalapeño pepper, chopped
2 (14 oz.) cans black beans, drained
1 (14 oz.) can white beans, drained
1 (16 oz.) can pork and beans
½ c. brown sugar
½ c. ketchup
salt and pepper to taste
cayenne pepper (optional)

To begin, brown the beef and the onions. Add the remaining ingredients and roast for 1–2 hours at 300 degrees.

Cajun Recipes

Cajun food is one of the few true American foods. Its roots combine French basics, American Indian influences, and Mexican spicing. The result is a cuisine that's all its own. These are my favorite Cajun recipes. They may be different from some you have tried, because everyone has their own variation.

Voodoo Chicken
Blackened Meat
Jambalaya
Gumbo
Etifé

Voodoo Chicken

This is one of my favorite Cajun dishes. Beware, it is extremely spicy! I like to serve it with jasmine rice and corn on the cob.

¼ c. canola oil
¼ c. flour
2 large sweet onions, chopped
3 red bell peppers, veined, seeded, and chopped
1 (2–3 lb.) chicken, quartered
4 cloves garlic, minced
½ c. white grape juice
¼ c. cider vinegar
¼ c. Louisiana hot sauce (such as Tabasco, etc.)
2 tsp. cayenne pepper
2 tsp. tarragon
2 Tbsp. chopped parsley

Begin by creating a brick roux by heating the oil and flour together for 20–30 minutes at 300 degrees, whisking often. When it is done, it will turn a brick-red color. Add the onions and peppers. Sautee until the onions are clear. Add the chicken quarters and stir until browned. Add the remaining ingredients; broast at 300 degrees for 2–3 hours, adding liquid as necessary. Pull the meat from the bones and serve in the sauce.

Blackened Meat

This dish stems from Cajun roots and varies greatly from recipe to recipe. One point is universal—the spices used need to char in order to give the food a blackened flavor. This recipe goes well with rice, fried okra, or collard greens.

½ lb. bacon
1 tsp. coarse ground black pepper
1 red bell pepper, cored and seeded
½ tsp. cayenne pepper
1 tsp. molasses
1 small sharp onion, chopped
2 cloves garlic, minced
¼ c. crushed Ritz cracker or bread crumbs
2 lbs. meat, any type

Pre-cook bacon in the Dutch oven until crispy. Remove bacon and set aside. Do not discard grease. In a blender, blend bacon, black pepper, red pepper, cayenne, molasses, onion, garlic, and crackers. Heat up the Dutch oven and add a little oil to the bacon grease if needed. Cook the meat in the Dutch oven. After you have seared the first side, spread blackened paste liberally on the seared part of the steak. Do the same on the other side. Cover and broast for 10–15 minutes at 350 degrees, turning twice. Remove from the Dutch oven; place on paper towels to soak up a little of the oil from the blackened meat.

Jambalaya

This is a quintessential Cajun dish. It is a stand-alone dish; it's got everything in it!

- ¼ c. canola oil
- ¼ c. flour
- 1 lb. boneless skinless chicken, chopped
- ½ lb. fresh shrimp, veined and peeled
- ½ lb. smoked sausage, sliced
- 1 large sweet onion
- 4 cloves garlic, crushed
- ½ c. chopped celery tops
- ½ c. sliced carrots
- 1 red bell pepper, chopped
- 1 c. white grape juice
- 1 (14 oz.) can chicken broth
- 4 c. cooked jasmine rice

Begin by making a brick roux by cooking the oil and flour together at 300 degrees for 30 minutes, whisking often until it turns a brick-red color. Stir in the meat and vegetables slowly. Cook until the chicken is lightly browned. Add the grape juice and broth; roast for 20 minutes at 300 degrees. After 30 minutes, there should be liquid remaining. If not, add just enough water so there is visible liquid on the bottom. Stir in the rice and serve.

Gumbo

They say if it walks, swims, flies, or slithers, it can be made into gumbo. This is a Cajun favorite and can be served as a stand-alone soup or as a gravy over rice. Individual variations of gumbo are many. Feel free to experiment and create your own gumbo.

¼ c. oil
¼ c. flour
I large sweet onion, chopped
I c. chopped celery
I c. chopped carrots
I tsp. cayenne pepper
I lb. boneless skinless chicken, chopped
½ lb. smoked sausage, chopped
3 (14 oz.) cans chicken broth
juice from I lemon
½ c. chopped okra
2 tsp. filé (this can be found in the spice section of
    your grocery store; it is ground sassafras leaves)

Begin by making a brick roux by cooking the oil and flour together at 300 degrees for 30 minutes, whisking often until it turns a brick-red color. While the roux is hot, stir in all the vegetables except the okra. Add the meat and stir-fry until it's browned. Add the remaining ingredients, except the okra and filé. Roast at 300 degrees for 30–45 minutes. While hot, stir in the okra and filé.

Etifé

This is one of my favorite Cajun dishes, and it is simple to make. It can be made with any type of meat, but it is most common with crawfish, shrimp, or chicken. It can be eaten as a stand-alone soup or over rice as gravy.

¼ c. oil
¼ c. flour
I large sweet onion, chopped
2 lbs. meat of your choice
4 cloves garlic, minced
2 (14 oz.) cans chicken broth
2 tsp. cayenne pepper
I c. heavy cream

Begin by making a brown roux by cooking the oil and flour at 300 degrees for 15–20 minutes, or until the roux looks like milk chocolate. Stir in the onions and meat. Cook until the meat is browned. Add the remaining ingredients, except the cream. Roast at 300 degrees for about 30 minutes. At this point, you can thicken it with starch to achieve your desired thickness. Finish by slowly stirring in the cream.

Curries

Curries are common and varied, as curry is the staple flavor across the Middle East and Asia. The word curry means "blend of spices." In Indian cooking, it is seven specific spices, but other varieties of curries use more or less. Because they are so varied, I have limited my recipes to the two most common curries: Thai and Indian. Enjoy!

Masala
Khorma
Red Curry
Green Curry
Yellow Curry
Musaman Curry
Golden Cashew Khorma

Masala

There are two major types of curries made in India. The Masala is your basic curry. In areas where the Khorma is the special-occasion curry, many eat Masala every day. Curry dishes are best served with rice (specifically basmatti) and okra, green beans, or spinach.

1 large sweet onion, chopped
2 Tbsp. butter
6 Tbsp. mild curry powder
2–3 lbs. chicken, shrimp, or lamb
juice from 1 lemon
5 cloves garlic, minced
2 (14 oz.) cans chicken broth
2 bay leaves
starch to thicken
1½ c. plain yogurt

Begin by caramelizing the onion in the butter. Add the curry powder and the meat; stir-fry until the meat is lightly browned. Add all the remaining ingredients except the yogurt and starch. Roast for 45–60 minutes at 300 degrees. Slowly stir in the starch until you achieve the desired thickness. Stir in the yogurt.

Khorma

The Khorma curry is similar to the masala in style but is reserved as a fancier meal. Serve it the same way as the masala, but use only the best cuts of meat in Khorma.

1 large sweet onion, chopped
½ stick butter
6 Tbsp. hot curry powder
2–3 lbs. chicken, shrimp, or lamb, diced
4 cloves garlic, chopped
2 red bell peppers, veined, seeded, and diced
1 (14 oz.) can chicken broth
1 (14 oz.) can coconut milk
2 bay leaves
1 large tomato, diced
starch to thicken
1 c. plain yogurt

Begin by caramelizing the onion in the butter. Add the curry and meat, stir-frying until the meat is browned. Add the remaining ingredients except the yogurt and starch; roast for 1 hour at 300 degrees. Thicken with starch as desired. Slowly stir in the yogurt just before serving.

Red Curry

Thai curries are all very similar, each having just a slightly different taste. The red curry is generally the spiciest. It should be served over jasmine rice.

4 cloves garlic, minced
1 large tomato
2 red bell peppers
1 sprig basil
3 Tbsp. mild curry powder
2 (14 oz.) cans coconut milk
2 tsp. ground red pepper
1 large onion, chopped
2 Tbsp. butter
2–3 lbs. chicken, pork, or beef, cut into strips
3 c. vegetables, such as bamboo shoots, water chestnuts, snow peas, broccoli, or carrots
starch to thicken

Begin by pureeing in a blender the garlic, tomato, bell peppers, basil, curry powder, 1 can of coconut milk, and the ground red pepper. Set aside. Caramelize the onion in the butter. Stir in the meat and stir-fry until lightly browned. Add the puree; roast for 30 minutes at 300 degrees. Add the vegetables. Roast another 10–15 minutes. Thicken with starch. Slowly stir in the remaining can of coconut milk and serve.

Green Curry

This is the most aromatic of the Thai curries. Serve over jasmine rice.

2 sprigs basil
juice from 3 limes
1 green bell pepper, veined, seeded, and diced
2 (14 oz.) cans coconut milk, divided
1 c. green tea, prepared
2 Tbsp. mild curry powder
2 jalapeño peppers, veined and seeded
1 large sweet onion, chopped
2 Tbsp. butter
¼ c. green onion, chopped
2–3 lbs. chicken, pork, or beef
2 potatoes, cubed
1 c. broccoli
1 c. bamboo shoots
starch to thicken

Begin by pureeing basil, lime juice, bell pepper, 1 can coconut milk, green tea, curry powder, and jalapenos. In your Dutch oven, caramelize the sweet onion in the butter. Add the meat and stir-fry until browned. Slowly add the puree and potatoes. Roast for 30 minutes at 300 degrees. Add the vegetables and roast for 10–15 minutes more. Thicken with the starch; slowly stir in the remaining can of coconut milk and serve.

Yellow Curry

The yellow curry is the mildest of the Thai curries. Serve it over jasmine rice.

I large sweet onion, chopped
½ lb. cashews
2 Tbsp. butter
2–3 lbs. chicken, pork, or beef
I red or yellow bell pepper, veined, seeded, and
    chopped
2 Tbsp. mild curry powder
4 cloves garlic, minced
I sprig fresh basil
I (14 oz.) can coconut milk
2 c. fresh vegetables, such as bamboo shoots, water
    chestnuts, carrots, or broccoli
starch to thicken

Begin by caramelizing the onions and cashews in the butter. Add the meat and stir-fry until browned. Add the remaining ingredients except starch. Roast at 300 degrees for 30 minutes. Thicken with the starch.

Musaman Curry

Musaman curry takes on a really unique taste due to the combination of peanut oil and curry. In my opinion, this is a love-it or hate-it recipe. I happen to love the combo. Serve it over jasmine rice.

1 large sweet onion, chopped
½ lb. shelled peanuts
¼ c. peanut oil
2–3 lbs. chicken, pork, or beef
3 Tbsp. mild curry powder
4 cloves garlic, minced
2 Tbsp. Thai chili sauce
1 (14 oz.) can coconut milk
2 c. any vegetables of any type
2 potatoes, cubed
starch to thicken

Begin by caramelizing the onions and peanuts in the peanut oil. Add the meat and stir-fry until browned. Add the remaining ingredients, except for starch, and roast for 30–45 minutes at 300 degrees. Thicken with the starch and serve.

Golden Cashew Khorma

This is a region-specific Khorma. It is my favorite of the Indian curries. This recipe is a special treat, due to the cost of the cashews and golden raisins it requires.

1 c. golden raisins
1 c. white grape juice
1 large onion, chopped
1 lb. cashew halves
½ stick butter
6 Tbsp. mild curry powder
2–3 lbs. chicken, shrimp, or lamb, chopped
3 potatoe̶ ̶ ̶ ̶d
2 bay le̶
juice̶
1 ̶ ̶ ̶ ̶lk

for 30 m̶.
Add the cur̶
is browned. Ad̶
the starch. Roast fo̶
desired thickness. Slow̶,

̶rape juice
̶utter.
̶at

Italian Recipes

Most people think of Italian food as spaghetti and pizza, but it is a lot more than that. I've put together some authentic Italian recipes, as well as some most people are familiar with.

Chicken Risotto
Chicken Lasagna
Parmesan Chicken
Chicken Primavera
Traditional Lasagna
Tuscan Onion Soup
Chicken & Seafood in White Sauce

Chicken Risotto

This is a signature Italian dish. It is a little time-consuming to make but well worth it.

¼ c. olive oil
3 c. arborio rice
I medium sharp onion, finely chopped
2 c. white grape juice
4 (14 oz.) cans chicken broth
I lb. boneless skinless chicken, sliced
I sprig fresh basil
I c. cut asparagus or broccoli
2 c. Italian brown crimini mushrooms, chopped
juice from I lemon
I c. grated fresh parmesan cheese

To begin, heat up the olive oil in the bottom of your Dutch oven. Stir in the rice and onions; stir-fry until the rice becomes clear on the edges. Meanwhile, in a separate Dutch oven, simmer the grape juice and chicken broth at a low temperature (200–250 degrees). Pour in just enough of the grade juice–broth mixture to cover the rice. Roast at 250 degrees for 30–35 minutes, stirring often. Continue adding the grape juice–broth mixture to keep the level above the rice. Continue until the rice is tender and creamy. In a separate Dutch oven, stir-fry the chicken, basil, asparagus or broccoli, mushrooms, and lemon juice until the chicken is browned. Add to the the risotto. Roast for 5–10 minutes. Add the parmesan cheese.

Chicken Lasagna

This is a healthier, tasty alternative to the traditional lasagna.

2 boxes lasagna noodles
1½ lbs. chicken breasts, chopped
juice from 1 lemon
5 cloves garlic, minced
2 c. ricotta cheese
2 c. cottage cheese
3 c. shredded mozzarella cheese, divided
3 eggs, whipped
2 c. broccoli
1 (24 oz.) can marinara sauce

Soft-boil the noodles so they are pliable but not soft. Stir-fry the chicken in your Dutch oven with the lemon juice and garlic. In a separate bowl, mix the ricotta cheese, cottage cheese, 2 cups of mozzarella, and eggs. Add the chicken. Layer this mixture in the Dutch oven, starting with noodles, followed by the cheese-chicken mix, broccoli, marinara, and noodles. Repeat with remaining ingredients. Sprinkle the remaining 1 cup mozzarella on the top. Bake at 350 degrees for about 1 hour. Let stand 10–15 minutes before serving.

Parmesan Chicken

This is my kids' favorite way to have chicken. Serve this over noodles with marinara sauce and green vegetables.

6 boneless skinless chicken breasts
4 eggs
4 Tbsp. flour
2 c. Italian bread crumbs
I c. fresh grated parmesan cheese
6 slices mozzarella cheese

Begin by pounding the thick part of the chicken breast until the breast is relatively uniform in thickness. Whip the eggs and flour together. Roll the chicken breast in the egg and sprinkle with the bread crumbs and parmesan cheese. Heat up just enough oil to cover the bottom of your Dutch oven. When the oil reaches 350 degrees, add the chicken. Cover and cook for 5 minutes or until the bottom of the chicken is golden brown. Turn the breasts and place the cheese on top of the fillets. Cover and cook 5–7 minutes longer or until the other side is golden brown. Place on top of spaghetti noodles, cover with marinara sauce, and serve.

Chicken Primavera

This is a very easy recipe to make in your Dutch oven, and it serves a lot of people. It is best served over rice or noodles.

2 lbs. chicken breast fillets
6 cloves garlic, crushed
2 sprigs fresh basil, chopped
2 lemons, squeezed
1 c. cottage cheese
½ c. sour cream
2 c. asparagus or broccoli
1 c. mushrooms, chopped
2 tomatoes, chopped
3 c. grated mozzarella cheese

Heat just enough oil to make the bottom of your Dutch oven glossy. Lightly brown the chicken, garlic, and basil. Add the remaining ingredients except the mozzarella cheese. Mix well, sprinkle the mozzarella on top, and bake for 40–45 minutes at 350 degrees.

Traditional Lasagna

There is nothing quite like lasagna cooked in a Dutch oven. This is one of my favorite recipes.

2 (12 oz.) pkgs. lasagna noodles
3 c. ricotta cheese
I c. cottage cheese
½ c. chopped green onion
4 eggs, whipped
I lb. sweet Italian sausage
6 cloves garlic, minced
4 c. grated mozzarella cheese
I (24 oz.) can marinara sauce

Begin by soft boiling the noodles so they are pliable but not soft. In a bowl, mix the ricotta cheese, cottage cheese, green onions, and eggs. Chop and cook the sausage. Layer the ingredients, starting with the noodles, followed by the cheese mix, sausage, garlic, marinara, and then mozzarella cheese. Repeat with remaining ingredients. Finish by sprinkling the remaining mozzarella cheese on top. Bake for 45–60 minutes at 350 degrees. Let the lasagna stand for 10–15 minutes before serving.

Tuscan Onion Soup

This soup brings out the best of the Tuscan region of Italy. It is best as a part of a large meal but works well as a stand-alone dish.

1 large sweet onion, chopped
2 Tbsp. olive oil
½ lb. boneless skinless chicken, chopped
4 cloves garlic, sliced
2 c. white grape juice
2 red bell peppers, seeded, veined, and sliced
4 Roma tomatoes, chopped
½ c. brown crimini mushrooms
3 (14 oz.) cans chicken broth
starch to thicken
1 c. cream

Begin by browning the onions in the olive oil in your Dutch oven. Add the chicken and garlic; stir-fry until the chicken is lightly brown. Add the remaining ingredients except the starch and cream. Roast at 300 degrees for 30–40 minutes. Thicken with starch. Slowly stir in the cream.

Chicken & Seafood
in White Sauce

This is my all-time favorite Italian recipe. This goes great over fresh noodles of any sort, though angel hair or fettuccine work best.

I lb. boneless skinless chicken breasts, chopped
½ lb. fresh bay scallops
½ stick butter
4 cloves garlic
2 c. white grape juice
2 red bell peppers, seeded, veined and chopped
2 c. broccoli crowns, cut bite-size
2 Tbsp. chopped green onions
I c. brown crimini mushrooms (optional)
I sprig fresh basil, chopped
juice from I lemon
starch to thicken
I c. cream

Begin by cooking the chicken, scallops, butter, and garlic in your Dutch oven until chicken and scallops are lightly browned. Add the grape juice and vegetables. Cover and roast for 15 minutes. Add the basil and lemon juice, thicken with the starch, and slowly stir in the cream. Serve over noodles with freshly grated parmesan cheese.

Asian Recipes

I could fill an entire book full of Asian recipes, there are so many. These are my own personal favorites. To create a true stir-fry, all your meat and vegetables should be bite-sized and uniform. That way it will all be done at the same time.

Sweet and Sour
Sesame Chicken
Cashew Chicken
Beef and Broccoli
Kung Pao Chicken
Beef with Snow Peas
Beef Tips in Oyster Sauce

Sweet & Sour

This is the traditional sweet and sour, not the deep-fried variety you see at most Chinese restaurants. Serve this over rice with stir-fried vegetables.

2 lbs. chicken or pork, chopped
¼ c. flour
4 Tbsp. sesame oil
1 large sweet onion, chopped
¼ c. chopped green onion
1 (20 oz.) can pineapple chunks with juice
juice from 1 lemon
¼ c. honey or brown sugar

Begin by rolling the meat in the flour. Heat up the oil in your Dutch oven. Vigorously stir-fry the meat and the sweet onions until well browned. Add the remaining ingredients. Roast for 15 minutes at 350 degrees, stirring occasionally. Let stand covered at least 5 minutes before serving.

Sesame Chicken

This sticky-sweet recipe is a classic. Serve over rice with stir-fried vegetables.

¼ c. sesame oil
4 Tbsp. sesame seeds
1½–2 lbs. boneless skinless chicken breasts, chopped
½ c. flour
1 tsp. ginger
½ tsp. cayenne pepper
¼ c. honey

Begin by heating up the sesame oil in the bottom of your Dutch oven. Stir-fry the sesame seeds and chicken. In a bowl, mix the flour, ginger, and cayenne. Slowly add to the Dutch oven, stirring constantly. Cover and roast for 10 minutes at 350 degrees. Slowly stir in the honey. Let stand for 5 minutes before serving.

Cashew Chicken

Cashew Chicken is one of the all-time favorite stir-fries. Serve over long grain rice.

1 lb. boneless chicken breast
1 large sweet onion, chopped
½ lb. cashew halves
2 Tbsp. butter
½ c. chopped celery
1 c. chopped broccoli
½ c. bamboo shoots or water chestnuts
¼ c. soy sauce
1 tsp. ground ginger
1 (14 oz.) can chicken broth
starch to thicken

Begin by stir-frying the chicken, onion, and cashews in the butter. When the chicken is lightly browned, add the vegetables and stir-fry for 2–3 minutes. Add the remaining ingredients except for starch. Cover and roast for 10 minutes at 350 degrees. Thicken with the starch.

Beef & Broccoli

This is undoubtedly the most famous stir-fry. Serve it over long grain rice or, for a different twist, try it over chow mein noodles.

1 lb. beef steak, cut into thin strips
1 large sweet onion, chopped
2 c. broccoli florets, cut into bite-sized pieces
1 c. sliced carrots
4 Tbsp. sesame oil
¼ c. flour
½ c. soy sauce
1 (14 oz.) can chicken broth, divided

Begin by stir-frying the beef, onions, broccoli, and carrots in the sesame oil. When the meat is browned, stir in the flour until everything is coated. Add the soy sauce and half the chicken broth. Cover and roast for 10–15 minutes at 350 degrees. Add broth to reach desired thickness.

Kung Pao Chicken

This is a dish most people are familiar with from Chinese restaurants. Serve it over long grain rice.

¼ c. peanut oil
1 large sharp onion, sliced into half rings
½ lb. salted peanuts
1 red bell pepper, seeded, veined, and chopped
2 jalapeño peppers, seeded, veined, and chopped
1 lb. chicken breast, cut into thin strips
2 c. zucchini, cubed
¼ c. soy sauce
5 Tbsp. oyster sauce
½ tsp. ground red pepper

To begin, heat up the peanut oil in your Dutch oven. Stir-fry the onion, peanuts, peppers, chicken, and zucchini. When the chicken is lightly browned, add the soy and oyster sauces and ground red pepper. Cover and roast 10 minutes at 350 degrees. Stir well before serving.

Beef with Snow Peas

This is one of my favorite stir-fries. Serve it over long grain rice.

1 lb. beef steak, cut into thin strips
1 large sweet onion, chopped
1 lb. snow peas, ends clipped
2 Tbsp. oil
1 tsp. ginger
¼ c. soy sauce
¼ c. oyster sauce

Stir-fry the meat, onions, and snow peas in the oil. When the meat is lightly browned, add the ginger, soy sauce, and oyster sauce. Cover and roast for 10 minutes at 350 degrees. Let stand 3–5 minutes.

Beef Tips
in Oyster Sauce

This is a stir-fry spin-off with no vegetables. It is a quick, easy, and tasty dish when you want an Asian-style meal without the hassle. I recommend serving this over rice, but it goes equally well with steamed new potatoes.

2 lbs. beef steaks, cut into strips
¼ stick butter
½ c. oyster sauce
1 tsp. hot sauce of choice (Tabasco, Tapatio, Cholu-
**   lu, etc.)**

Brown beef strips in butter until lightly browned. Add the remaining ingredients, then cover and broast for 15–20 minutes.

Southwestern Recipes

At home, I cook Southwest recipes than any other type because, growing up in Utah, it is the type of food we ate the most. Besides Cajun, Southwest is the only other true American cuisine.

Pazole
Black Molé
Easy Fajitas
Barbecued Brisket
Mesquite Chicken
Chicken Enchiladas
Southwest Beef Tips
Chipotle Ranch Chicken

Pazole

Pazole is my favorite Mexican dish. It is great as a stand-alone dish. I like to garnish it with fresh-squeezed limes, chopped onions, chopped cabbage, cilantro, and fresh tortillas.

I large sweet onion, chopped
2 Tbsp. oil
1–2 lbs. pork, any type
I (32 oz.) can white hominy (found in some grocery
    stores and Mexican markets)
4 cloves garlic, crushed
I (24 oz.) can crushed tomatoes
¼ c. white vinegar
4 Tbsp. Mexican oregano
2 Tbsp. New Mexico chile powder
4 Tbsp. brown sugar
3 (14 oz.) cans chicken broth
2 bay leaves

Begin by caramelizing the onions in the oil. Add the pork and lightly brown the meat. Add the remaining ingredients and roast for at least 1 hour and no more than 2 hours.

Black Molé

Molé has a taste all its own. There are several regional versions of molé all over Mexico. The black or dark molé is probably the most popular. Serve this Tex-Mex style with tortillas, beans, and rice.

1 (2–3 lb.) chicken, quartered
5 Tbsp. extra dark cocoa powder
1 large sweet onion, chopped
3 jalapeño peppers, veined, seeded, and sliced
2 tsp. New Mexico chile powder
1 (14 oz.) can tomato sauce
3 Tbsp. honey or brown sugar
1 (14 oz. can) chicken broth
3 Tbsp. creamy peanut butter

Begin by lightly browning the chicken quarters, cocoa, and onions. Add the remaining ingredients and broast or bake for 60–90 minutes at 350 degrees. I like to pull the meat and let it stand in the molé for a few minutes before serving.

Easy Fajitas

This recipe is great for good fajitas when you are in a hurry or don't feel like cooking a gourmet meal. It's usually served Tex-Mex style in a flour tortilla with beans and rice.

- **1 large sweet onion**
- **1 large red bell pepper**
- **1 lb. beef, chicken, or pork, cut into strips**
- **1 McCormick's fajita seasoning mix**
- **¼ cube butter**

Cut onion and pepper into ¼-inch strips, taking care to remove the veins and seeds in the pepper. Set aside. Lightly brown the meat in the Dutch oven. When the meat is lightly brown, add the peppers and onions, and then stir-fry until the onions are clear. Add the seasoning mix and butter. Cover and broast for 10 minutes at 300 degrees.

Barbecue Brisket

This is the dish that made Texas famous. Though this is traditionally slow-cooked in a smokehouse, the Dutch oven works very well. This dish goes great with potatoes and corn for a main meal, and it works as a sandwich too.

1 (3–5 lb.) beef brisket
12 oz. apple juice
1 (14 oz.) can beef broth
1 large sweet onion, chopped
5 Tbsp. Liquid Smoke, mesquite flavor
2 c. barbecue sauce
4 Tbsp. brown sugar

Begin by browning the brisket very well on all sides. If the brisket won't fit flat in the Dutch oven, cut it in half or quarters. When the meat is browned, lay it fat-side up, add a little of the apple juice and broth, and then broast or bake with the onions and Liquid Smoke for 4–5 hours at 250–275 degrees. Check it every 30 minutes, adding the juice and broth a little at a time. When the meat can be pulled apart easily, remove from the Dutch oven. Add the barbecue sauce, brown sugar, and whatever juice and broth is left. Slice the meat cross-grain and return to the sauce. Let stand for 5–10 minutes in the sauce before serving.

Mesquite Chicken

This easy recipe is one of my favorites. This recipe goes well Tex-Mex style with beans, rice, and tortillas. It also goes great with potatoes.

- 2 lbs. chicken breasts
- 2 Tbsp. oil
- 1 pkg. McCormick's dry mesquite marinade
- 2 cloves garlic, sliced
- 1 red bell pepper, veined, seeded, and chopped
- 1 large sweet onion, chopped
- 2 Tbsp. butter
- 3 Tbsp. Liquid Smoke, mesquite flavor
- ¼ c. Worcestershire sauce

Begin by browning the chicken breasts in a little oil. Generously sprinkle the mesquite marinade on the chicken; add the garlic, peppers, onions, butter, and Liquid Smoke. Cover and broast for 15 minutes at 300 degrees. Add the Worcestershire sauce and broast another 5–7 minutes.

Chicken Enchiladas

This is a recipe I make when I have some leftover chicken. If you don't have leftovers, you can make some chicken fresh as well. Serve this Tex-Mex style with beans and rice.

1 small sharp onion, chopped
2 Tbsp. butter
1½ lbs. boneless chicken, chopped
1 c. green salsa (I prefer Herdez salsa verde)
3 tsp. Liquid Smoke, mesquite flavored
2 tsp. New Mexico chile powder
1 pkg. corn tortillas
3 c. shredded Colby jack cheese

Begin by caramelizing the onion in the butter. Stir in the chicken, salsa, Liquid Smoke, and chile powder. Fill the center of each tortilla, roll it up, and place it in your Dutch oven. Cover the enchiladas with the cheese, then drizzle some salsa on top. Bake or broil for 10–15 minutes at 350–375 degrees until the cheese is fully melted and beginning to brown. Let the enchiladas stand for 5 minutes before serving.

Southwest Beef Tips

This is a very easy recipe when you are in the mood for some quick tacos. I like to eat this as a taco or fajita with beans and rice.

1 large sweet onion, chopped
4 Tbsp. butter
2 lbs. beef steak, cut into thin strips
4 cloves garlic, sliced
2 red bell peppers, veined, seeded, and chopped
juice from 2 limes
1 pkg. McCormick's Southwest dry marinade

Begin by caramelizing the onions in the butter. Stir in the beef until it is lightly browned. Add the remaining ingredients and broast for 15 minutes at 350 degrees. Stir well before serving.

Chipotle Ranch Chicken

This is a classic Southwest recipe that goes great with potatoes and corn.

2–3 lbs. chicken, any type
2 Tbsp. butter
1 pkg. dry ranch dressing mix
1 (3–4 oz.) can Chipotle peppers
1 Anaheim pepper, seeded, veined, and chopped
1 red bell pepper, seeded, veined, and chopped
1 (14 oz.) can chicken broth, divided
½ c. sour cream

Begin by browning the chicken in the butter. Add the ranch mix, peppers, and half of the broth. Broast for 15–20 minutes at 350 degrees. Add the remaining chicken broth. Broast for another 15–20 minutes. Stir in the sour cream and serve.

Dutch Oven Classics

I can't have a Dutch oven cookbook without including some classic recipes. These are my variation on some recipes most people know.

McGuiness Stew
Chicken & Stuffing
Beef Tips & New Potatoes
Classic Dutch Oven Dinner
French Onion Chicken & Rice

McGuiness Stew

This is my favorite breakfast Dutch oven meal. I make it quite often for dinner as well.

2 c. cubed ham
1½ lbs. potatoes
2 Tbsp. butter
12 eggs
¼ c. medium salsa
½ lb. shredded cheddar cheese

Begin by browning the ham and potatoes in the butter. Cover and roast for 10–15 minutes at 300 degrees or until the potatoes are tender. Do not stir after it is browned. In a separate bowl, whip the eggs, salsa, and cheese. Pour into the Dutch oven and stir until the eggs are about halfway set up. Cover and let stand about 5 minutes off the heat. Stir for 2–3 minutes and serve.

Chicken & Stuffing

This is a classic Dutch oven meal. The trick is cooking all of it together in the same pot. For the top layer, you can use the stuffing recipe provided, your own recipe, or a prepared box mix. Serve this with mashed potatoes for a hearty Thanksgiving-like meal any time.

Bottom Layer:
1 (2–3 lb.) chicken, quartered
2 Tbsp. butter
1 tsp. sage
salt to taste
1 tsp. black pepper
1 (14 oz.) can chicken broth
½ lb. thick-sliced bacon (smoked)
1 bunch fresh whole spinach leaves

Top Layer:
6 c. dried or stale bread chunks
½ c. sliced sweet onion, chopped
½ c. chopped celery
2 tsp. sage
1 Tbsp. chopped parsley
Salt and pepper to taste
2 eggs, whipped

Begin by browning the chicken in the butter. Add the seasonings and broth. Lay the bacon and spinach across the top of the chicken. Mix all top-layer ingredients (or prepare alternate stuffing) and layer on top of the spinach. Broast 1–2 hours at 300 degrees.

Beef Tips
& New Potatoes

This has always been a classic Dutch oven camping dish.

2–3 lbs. beef, cut into cubes
2 Tbsp. butter
1 medium sharp onion, chopped
2–3 lbs. small red potatoes
2 (14 oz.) cans beef broth
2 tsp. black pepper
2 Tbsp. honey
starch to thicken

Start by stir-frying the beef and onions in the butter. Add the remaining ingredients. Roast or broast for 60–90 minutes or until the beef is tender. Thicken to a gravy using starch.

Classic
Dutch Oven Dinner

I couldn't do a Dutch oven cookbook without giving my recipe for the classic Dutch oven dinner.

1 large sweet onion, chopped
½ stick butter
2 lbs. cubed beef chuck
3 c. sliced carrots
4 c. cubed potatoes
1 (12 oz.) can cola
2 bay leaves
1 tsp. cayenne pepper
1 (14 oz.) can beef broth
2 c. mushrooms
¼ c. Worcestershire sauce
starch to thicken

Begin by caramelizing the onion in the butter. Add the beef. Stir-fry until it is browned. Add the carrots, potatoes, cola, bay leaves, cayenne, and broth. Roast or broast at 300 degrees for 1½–2 hours. Add the mushrooms and roast for another 10 minutes. Add the Worcestershire sauce and thicken to gravy using the starch.

French Onion Chicken & Rice

This is a recipe my dad made for us a lot growing up. It tastes great and is easy to make.

1½ c. rice
2 pkg. Lipton French onion soup mix
4–5 chicken breasts, bone-in with skin

Combine all ingredients in your Dutch oven, placing the chicken on top. Roast or broast at 300 degrees for about 1 hour or until the rice is tender and the moisture is absorbed. If the liquid is gone and the rice is crunchy, add a small amount of liquid until the rice is tender.

Conclusion

Dutch oven cooking is becoming more and more popular every year. Practice often and soon you will be preparing dishes that will impress. You can almost always find Dutch oven cook-offs if you look. Join one and try it out! Even if you don't think that you can win, there's a great bonding that happens among the competitors. You can learn some new ideas that will help you on your next outing.

How could I do a Dutch oven cookbook full of main courses without leaving you with dessert?

Matt's Easy Peach Cobbler

I know everyone has their own recipe for Peach Cobbler. It's probably the most famous Dutch oven dessert. I have tried most of them, and this is far and away the easiest to make and the best tasting. Whatever you do, do not line your dutch oven with foil! The cobbler won't cook right, and the Dutch oven cleans up just fine on its own.

> **2 (32 oz.) cans peach halves in light syrup**
> **½ c. cranberry juice**
> **½ tsp. salt**
> **1 tsp. nutmeg**
> **2 tsp. real vanilla extract**
> **1 box yellow cake mix**
> **5 Tbsp. butter**

Drain the syrup out of one of the cans. Pour the contents of both cans into the bottom of your Dutch oven. Add the cranberry juice, salt, nutmeg, and vanilla. Do not stir. Sprinkle the yellow cake mix over the peaches. Slice the butter extremely thin and lay the slices on top of the cake mix, spreading them out evenly. Broast the cobbler for 30 minutes at 325 degrees. Increase the amount of coals on the top and bake for 10–15 minutes more at 350 degrees. Check often to make sure that the crust does not burn. When the cobbler is done, it will be browned in places on the top. Remove from the heat, and let stand covered for at least 30 minutes. (I know it's hard to wait, but it's so much better after it sets up.)

About the Author

Matt Pelton grew up in a small farming community in central Utah where Dutch oven cooking was a part of every town event. Matt started cooking for his family at the age of twelve. At the age of eighteen, he began to study cooking techniques from chefs from around the world. He learned that cooking has very little to do with recipes and a lot to do with processes. He has spent the last thirteen years learning these processes and teaching them to anyone who wanted to learn. Matt's specialty has been outdoor cooking and cooking wild game. His first book, From Mountaintop to Tabletop, has helped many hunters learn the skills for cooking wild game. Matt has also had many magazine articles published and has been a presenter at the International Sportsman's Expo, teaching seminars in outdoor cooking. Matt currently resides in Provo, Utah, with his wife, Katie, and their three children, Megan, 7, Tristan, 5, and Braxton, 1.